The Government of American Cities

A Program of Democracy

By
Horace E. Deming

A Study of Municipal Organization and of the
Relation of the City to the State

Also a Reprint of The Municipal Program of
The National Municipal League

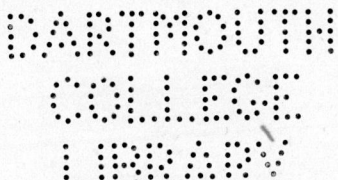

G. P. Putnam's Sons
New York and London
The Knickerbocker Press

COPYRIGHT, 1909
BY
HORACE E. DEMING

Published, March, 1909
Reprinted, October, 1909; April, 1911

The Knickerbocker Press, New York

The author is entirely responsible for the statements of fact and of opinion contained in this book, but he gratefully acknowledges the great assistance he has received from the criticisms of Prof. W. B. Munro of Harvard University, Prof. John A. Fairlie of the University of Michigan, Dr. Delos F. Wilcox of New York, and Mr. Charles Richardson and Mr. Clinton Rogers Woodruff of Philadelphia, who read the entire work in manuscript; from Dr. Frederick A. Cleveland of the Bureau of Municipal Research, and Dr. Milo R. Maltbie of the Public Service Commission, New York City, and Dr. W. B. Bailey of Yale University, who examined parts of the book. Messrs. Munro, Fairlie, and Wilcox have placed the author under yet further obligations by reading and criticizing the proofs of the book as it passed through the press.

H. E. D.

PREFACE

THE failure of city government in the United States is not a failure of democracy.

On the contrary it is and it has been due to the failure to apply to city government in America the same democratic principles that, so far as they have been applied, are the cause of good government in state and nation.

The nearest approach to a government representative of and accountable to the governed is found in successfully governed cities. This book aims to show that the misgovernment of American cities is due not to the defects of democratic principles (nor to any dissimilarity in the principles of correct city government and the principles of civil government generally), but to an utter failure to apply them; that the successful conduct of city government, the world over, has been in direct proportion to the application of the fundamental principles of democracy, and that the experience of European cities has demonstrated that the complexity of city government is in the variety and magnitude of the interests affected by it and not in the nature of the principles involved.

So far as the writer is aware, no book has been written about American city government from this point of view. The following pages aim to show that it is the correct point of view, both as a deduction from sound political philosophy and as a demonstration from the actual municipal experience of Europe and America.

New York, January, 1909.

CONTENTS

PAGE

CHAPTER I.

The City Problem in Europe and the United States 1

CHAPTER II.

The English Municipal System . . . 13

CHAPTER III.

The Domination of Cities by State Legislatures in the United States 26

CHAPTER IV.

City Government in England and the United States Contrasted 34

CHAPTER V.

The Effect of the Political Doctrines of "Checks and Balances" and "Short Terms of Office" 50

CHAPTER VI.

The Changing Popular Attitude toward Certain Political Doctrines and Practices which

	PAGE
have Made Bad City Government Inevitable in the United States	61

CHAPTER VII.

Growth of the Popular Determination to Have a City Government Responsible to its Citizens	79

CHAPTER VIII.

City Government is Government	114

CHAPTER IX.

The Relation of the City to the State	125

CHAPTER X.

The Relation of the City to its Citizens	140

CHAPTER XI.

Pre-requisites to the Self-Government of Cities	153

CHAPTER XII.

How the Opportunity for Local Self-Government must be Won	171

CHAPTER XIII.

Importance of Electoral Methods in Securing Real Local Self-Government	178

CHAPTER XIV.

A City's Charter	188

Contents

CHAPTER XV.
The City the Battle-ground of Democracy . 192

CHAPTER XVI.
Democracy and Efficiency 198

Discussion of the Municipal Program of The National Municipal League . . . 203

Text of the Municipal Program of The National Municipal League 241

Index 305

Index to the Municipal Program . . . 318

The Government of American Cities

CHAPTER I

THE CITY PROBLEM IN EUROPE AND THE UNITED STATES

WHENEVER a country is sufficiently advanced in civilization to develop among its inhabitants a considerable traffic in the products of their industries, portions of the population will tend to mass in convenient centres of distribution and exchange. Especially is this the case when the traffic is large, not only among the inhabitants of the same country but between them and the people of other countries. This massing of the people at centres of distribution and exchange creates cities, and the better the facilities of transportation, the greater is the traffic and the more numerous and more populous are the cities. Cities thus spring into existence in obedience to a fundamental economic law. Whatever, therefore, increases the subjects of traffic and the facilities of transportation is certain to add to the number and to the population of cities.

Toward the end of the eighteenth century, began the use of steam as a source of power. Since that time, steam has multiplied, almost beyond reckoning, the products of human industry, has increased in numberless ways the ease and speed of transportation, and has been constantly creating new highways for commerce. It was inevitable that under the impulse of steam-power cities should grow rapidly in number and make constant gains in population over rural regions. During the last twenty-five years, electricity has added its potent influence and the tendency of the population cityward has been still further quickened. Nothing is more certain than that in all countries where steam and electricity are in general use—improving and increasing the facilities of transportation, multiplying the subjects of traffic, enlarging and emphasizing the influence of the factory method of production—a very large proportion of their inhabitants will be city-dwellers. The phenomenon of city growth has not been an isolated one peculiar to the United States but has been common to all progressive peoples. The redistribution of the population, its massing in the centres of manufacture, distribution, and exchange, has been even more striking in Germany and England than in the United States.[1]

In the countries of Western Europe at the opening of the nineteenth century, very little effective attention had been paid to the matter of city government. Speaking generally, it was everywhere unsatisfactory. In some of them it was scandalously inefficient, and, in very many instances, it was not only grossly incompetent but notoriously and to all appearances hopelessly corrupt. Yet by the year 1880, when the people of the United States were beginning to be conscious that they had a grave city problem, Germany, Holland, Belgium, France, and England each had already found a way to provide its cities with honest, progressive, and efficient city government. Each of these countries had a national government unlike that of any of the others; in no two were the political habits and traditions of the people the same. Each country had proceeded in its own way and followed its own methods; their municipal systems were widely divergent, yet their cities were and are well governed. It is clear that difference in form or structural plan will not account for this result. There must have been in these different countries and cities the recognition and observance of basic principles upon which successful city government must rest.

[1] Full details regarding this movement may be found in A. F. Weber's *Growth of Cities in the Nineteenth Century* (New York, 1899).

Let us attempt to discover those principles.

Every government, of whatever kind or form, must, in order to act at all, have some organ or organs whose function is to determine how it shall act, that is, its policy, *e. g.*, whether a tax shall be laid upon imports, a system of highways be established, a postal service be maintained, the navy be enlarged, harbors improved, transportation regulated, what shall be the monetary standard, what the powers of banking institutions shall be,—to mention only a few of the numberless questions of public policy. On such questions, there are always divergent opinions. They give rise to divisive political issues, and those who take part in deciding them frequently become strong partisans. This is the policy-determining or political side of the conduct of the government.

But when once the policy has been determined upon, the management of the custom-houses, the collection of the taxes, the actual construction of the highways, the management of the postal service, the building of the ships, the enforcement of the transportation regulations, the supervision of the banking companies, the maintenance of the monetary standard involve no divisive political issue. This is the purely administrative or, as it might be called, business side of the conduct of government. It is not the opinions of the members of its administrative service upon matters of govermental policy which are important, but their honesty, zeal, intelligence, and efficiency in the performance of the enterprise which the government has decided to undertake. Whether the members of its administrative service have or have not these qualities is often of great importance to the government in determining wisely questions of policy, but the decision of questions of governmental policy is no part of the duties of the members of its purely administrative service.

This distinction between the policy-determining, or political, and the purely administrative side of government finds a close analogy in the conduct of every large business enterprise. The conductors, traffic managers, accountants, ticket agents, brakemen, track-walkers, superintendents of a railway company, do not decide whether or not the company's resources shall be used to extend the trackage, to build new bridges, to enlarge terminals; or whether additional lines shall be leased, or the capital stock increased, or more bonds issued. Their views on these matters of policy are purely personal and have nothing to do with the performance of their duties as members of the company's administrative staff. The engineer whose approval or disapproval of the company's policy affected in even the slightest degree the quality of his engineering work would be considered, and very rightly, as unfitted for his position.

The importance of recognizing this fundamental difference between the policy-determining and the administrative sides of government and of keeping the two quite distinct in its practical conduct is especially marked in the case of a city government, for nine tenths of its activities are on the administrative side. In the practical conduct of city government, therefore, the quality of its administrative service is of a consequence very difficult to exaggerate. Some way must be found to keep politics out of its administrative service, if the government is to be conducted successfully. Politics in the administrative service of a city government is certain to demoralize that service. From any logical point of view, to permit politics in the administrative service of a city is precisely as absurd as would be the attempt to run a railroad by selecting or retaining trainmen, clerks, freight-agents, and engineers according to their views upon the various questions of policy that it was the function of the directors of the company to decide.

No one will dispute the correctness of these statements or the soundness of their logic so long as we confine ourselves to the realm of pure reason. But can they be put in practice in this busy world which does not occupy itself much with theorizing, and in which governmental and every other business is conducted not according to any counsel of perfection but after any practical fashion which seems most available at the moment? The answer is found in the history of the city governments of Germany, Belgium, Holland, France, and England. That these countries in the practical conduct of their city governments have each recognized and applied these basic principles is one of the chief reasons why Dresden, Brussels, Amsterdam, Lyons, and Manchester, though each has a form of government widely different from all the others, is a well governed municipality.

Bulky volumes would be required to describe the working machinery of the various city governments in Western Europe. But the essential and controlling facts that explain why, though differing so widely in governmental framework, they are nevertheless alike in being well governed do not require lengthy statement.

City government, like all government, must perform two distinct functions:

1. It must have a policy adapted to the needs of the people governed; and since the primary purpose of city government is to satisfy the local needs, the policy of a city government must be adapted to the needs of the city.

2. It must provide a city administrative service manned by competent persons selected and retained with no reference to their views as to the public policy of the city government or any other government.

In Germany, in France, in England, in Holland and in Belgium, the policy which controls the government of a city is not an imperial or national or other external policy, but a local policy adapted to the local needs of the city; the officials of the city's administrative service are selected because of their honesty and competence, and the limit of their tenure is determined by their efficiency and good behavior. Thus two basic principles which lie at the foundation of the successful conduct of any government and more especially of city government are not only recognized theoretically but are practically applied and enforced. This is not due to the compulsion of superior authority, or in obedience to specially enacted statutes. Nor is there any formal prohibition of the performance of policy-determining and administrative functions by the same public officers. It happens more often than otherwise that the local legislature—and there is always a local legislature—in addition to its political policy-determining functions performs through its committees important administrative functions as well. It is not by virtue of enacting into law any special plan or scheme that these cities are well governed; there is a wide variety in the formal frameworks of their governments. But there is not one of these countries which has not discovered two prerequisites to the solution of its city problem: that each city should be governed according to the policy which suits its local needs; and should have a trustworthy, competent, and non-political administrative service. And each country in its own way has successfully applied the discovery.

These countries have also recognized and successfully applied another important principle—namely, that city government is *government* and must therefore be clothed with power to satisfy the local needs of the city and that, in order to decide how it should exercise its local power, it must have some policy-determining organ or organs of its own.

In these countries there is no granting of powers to the city followed by curtailing or perhaps taking them away altogether. And each city government has a local legislature locally elected by the qualified electors of the city in local campaigns when members of the local legislature are practically the only elective officers to be chosen. The superior authority of the state, if there is occasion for its exercise, is exercised through administrative methods, and is kept within well defined limits.

To sum up, however divergent the cities of Western Europe may be in their governmental form and framework, in their practical working:

(1) Each is a local government clothed with powers to satisfy the local needs;

(2) Each is a local government conducted according to a local policy locally determined;

(3) Each determines its local policy through the election of a local legislature in a local political campaign turning upon local political issues;

(4) Each has practically no elected city officials except members of the city legislature;

(5) Each has an administrative service, the members of which obtain and hold their positions irrespective of their opinions on either local or national political issues;

(6) Each exercises its local powers without arbitrary interference from outside authority;

(7) The superior authority of the central government, when there is occasion for its assertion, is exercised through administrative methods.

There is not one of these principles which has not been directly violated or heedlessly disregarded in the practical conduct of city government in the United States. The conclusion is irresistible. Where these principles have been applied, city government has been successful; where they have been violated or disregarded, city government has been a failure. Whether tested by European or by American municipal experience, the all-important character of these principles has been established. They are the basal underlying principles of successful city government.

The enemies of democracy can find no consolation or comfort in the fact that the cities of Europe have been well governed and the cities of the United States ill governed. For what constitutes democratic government? Not a particular form or structural plan, but the fact that the government represents the governed; that it is conducted according to policies which conform to the prevailing public opinion, deliberately formed and authentically expressed by those subject to the action of the government; that the persons clothed with governmental powers are readily and surely accountable to the governed for the use of those powers. Tested by these standards, the cities of Western Europe are much nearer to municipal democracy than the cities of the United States.

The European city is largely a self-governing community; the American city has been a subject community. In Europe the city has a local government clothed with large powers (and many European cities have governments clothed with all the powers) to meet the local needs of the city; these powers are exercised in accordance with a local public policy locally determined, and are exercised by local public officials responsible and responsive to the local electorate. The city in the United States has been a local government with inadequate power to meet the local needs of the city; and has had no effective means of compelling the exercise of even this limited power in accordance with local public policy locally determined; nor has the local electorate been able to enforce responsibility for the conduct of its local public affairs.

In brief, the successful city governments of Europe have been striking illustrations of the beneficent effects of a practical, even if by no means complete, application of the principles of democracy to local government; and the city governments of the United States have been striking examples of the evils that result from the attempt to conduct local government in open and flagrant violation of the basic principles of democracy. Herein lies the true explanation of the contrasting municipal experience of Europe and the United States. Not the application of democratic principles but the disregard of them is the cause of municipal misrule in the United States. It is the constantly clearer discernment of this fact during the last twenty-five years that gives assurance that here also the cities will in time be well governed.

CHAPTER II

THE ENGLISH MUNICIPAL SYSTEM [1]

TO a citizen of the United States, the municipal history of England is perhaps more informing and suggestive than that of any other of the countries of Western Europe. It is not only that the political traditions and habits of the English people and of our own are derived from a common source, and that we thus understand the methods employed in England; but the municipal evils from which England was suffering when her present system of city government was established seventy years ago were even more grievous than those we are to-day confronting in the United States, and yet those evils disappeared under the operation of the Municipal Reform Act adopted in 1835. It is noteworthy, also, that there has

[1] For detailed information on the matters dealt with in this chapter, the reader may be referred to Redlich and Hirst's *Local Government in England* (2 vols., London, 1904); to Webb's *English Local Government* (3 vols., London, 1906–1908); to the chapters on municipal administration in Lowell's *Government of England* (2 vols., New York, 1908); and to Munro's *Government of European Cities* (New York, 1909), Chap. III.

been no change in principle or method since that act was adopted. The English system has been eminently stable. From time to time new laws have been passed upon the subject of municipal government, but these have served to strengthen the original act and to enlarge the area of its application. In 1882, the law of 1835 and these subsequent statutes were recast into a general municipal code compact in form and containing 269 sections.

In 1835 each English city had its special charter. There was the same bewildering variety of structural plan that is found in the United States. Misgovernment and inefficiency were universal. Corruption was very prevalent. In the conduct of city government the will of the governed found little and usually no expression.[1] To-day, more than one half of the inhabitants of England and Wales, exclusive of London which has a special government of its own, dwell in more than three hundred cities, large and small, each of which is to a marked extent a genuine self-governing community that conducts its local affairs successfully under the provisions of one general municipal corporations act. And, excluding London, this could have been said of every English city at any time since the system inaugurated by the Municipal Reform Act of

[1] See, for abundant evidence on these points, the *Report of the Royal Commission on Municipal Corporations*, in the *Parliamentary Papers for 1835*.

1835 was fairly established. This does not mean that each city is exactly like every other in the details of its administrative organization,—each city arranges these in its own discretion,—but it does mean that the English system of city government is at once simple and comprehensive, that it has successfully withstood the searching practical test of daily experience under every variety of circumstance for seventy years, and has proved itself admirably adapted at every stage of their growth to the needs of cities of widely varying characteristics, small and large, maritime and inland.

The fundamentals of the English Municipal Code, its ground plan, may be stated briefly. Each city is a corporation clothed with large local powers of government. These powers are exercised by a board, locally selected in the following manner: The city is ordinarily divided into districts, in each of which the qualified voters elect three members of the board, one each year for a term of three years. These elected members, called councillors, choose additional members of the board to the number of one third, called aldermen. The aldermen are chosen for a term of six years, and one half retire triennially. For example, if there are twelve councillors, these choose four aldermen, two each third year for a term of six years. The full board of councillors and aldermen is called the Council and chooses one of their own number—or an outsider, although this is not usual—as Mayor. The Mayor, save that he is titular president of the Council and is *ex officio* a magistrate, has no greater power than any other member. The Code requires the Council to choose a town clerk and a treasurer and to appoint from its own membership a "Watch Committee" to control local police matters.[1] Such other officials as may be desired or needed are appointed and removed and their salaries and tenures fixed by the Council, which also has full power to meet every need or phase of local administration.

In substance and in effect the English system commits the conduct of the local public affairs of each community to a central committee, or board selected by the locality to carry out the local will. There is no lack of politics or political partisanship under the system, but the politics are mainly local politics and the heat of the political campaigns is excited by local issues. The local election never occurs at the same time as any other election and there is only one elective office arousing any political interest, the councillorship.[2] The voter has therefore only to consider and decide upon the merits of candidates for this one office.

The election methods are very simple. The

[1] The Education Act of 1902 has also provided for an "Education Committee" to control the schools.

[2] Two auditors and two revising assessors are elected annually by the city at large.

candidate is nominated by filing with the town clerk a paper upon which one elector proposes, another elector seconds, and eight additional electors endorse the candidate. When there is no burning local issue it sometimes happens that only one such nominating paper is filed; in which case no formal election is held and the candidate named in the one nominating paper is declared elected. This has occurred very frequently. The honesty and purity of the electoral methods are amply safeguarded. The ballot is a secret official ballot printed at public expense and furnished the voter within the polling place. It contains the names of all the candidates alphabetically arranged under the title of the office, without any designation of the political parties to which the nominees belong. The voter goes into a private booth and marks his preference, then comes out of the booth and deposits his ballot with the election officer. The counting and canvassing of the ballots are admirably provided for.

In practice, the members of the Council who render conspicuously good service to the locality are sure of a long tenure. They are elected and re-elected term after term. Instances are numerous of members who have been in office continuously for twenty years or even longer.[1]

[1] See Professor F. J. Goodnow's article on "The British Municipality" in the recent *Report of the National Civic Federation* (3 vols., New York, 1907), vol. i.

The aldermen are usually men who have won previous distinction as councillors.

The opportunities afforded by membership in these local boards have from the beginning attracted men of eminent ability, and the English city commands the services of highly competent and public-spirited men in its Council. It has been natural, therefore, that the powers granted to cities in the original Municipal Reform Act have never been curtailed and that subsequent legislation has granted additional powers. There is now scarcely any matter of important local concern except poor relief which is not within the jurisdiction of the city Council.

There has been another and most important result. The men of ability and reputation, elected to these local boards and charged with full responsibility to the local electorate for the exercise of large powers that directly and vitally affect the local interests, have developed local administrative organizations based upon a thorough-going application of the merit principle in appointment, tenure, and promotion. This exclusion of politics from administration is the more noteworthy because it is due neither to any legal compulsion, nor to any formal or physical separation of the executive from the legislative department of the city government, nor to the mandate of any superior authority.

The Council of an English city through its committees directs the entire city administration.

The English Municipal System

It has complete power to organize the city's administrative service in any manner it chooses; decides into what departments that service shall be divided, establishes the jurisdiction of each, and fixes the duties, salaries, and tenures of the department officials. There is no administrative matter so large as to be beyond the scope of the Council's power or so minute as to escape its control. The Council has lacked neither the power nor the opportunity to use the administrative service for "political" ends; for the entire "patronage" of the public service of an English city is at the absolute disposal of its Council, every civil servant of the city is a subordinate of the Council without fixed term and removable at its pleasure, and no law prevents compelling every one of them to be an adherent of the political views held by the majority of the Council.

Neither has the Council been persuaded to keep the political and administrative sides of the city government thus entirely distinct because of any philosophical views on the nature of government and the differing nature of its political and administrative functions. The exclusion of politics from administration has been due to the fact that the members of the Council could be held personally accountable by the local electorate for the success or failure of the local government. History shows that the possession of power, for the use of which there is an easily enforceable accountability to the persons granting the power, stimulates its possessor to study the interests of those who have entrusted him with the power and who may take it away. This principle has found full play under the English Municipal Code. The members of the Council are put there by the local electorate to run the city government and, under the simple electoral system that has been described, cannot escape full responsibility for success or failure. The responsibility rests upon them and upon nobody else. It was inevitable, therefore, that the able men who constituted the Council of an English city should recognize that in the administrative service of a city, as of any other corporation of which they were the directors, the views and opinions of a member of the administrative staff upon questions of corporate policy are matters of indifference when the faithful and efficient performance of his administrative duties does not depend upon them. In the administrative service of the English city, the Council has seen to it, as a matter of plain business sense, that every official should be selected, retained, and promoted for efficiency and good conduct without reference to his political opinions. And this is true not merely of one English city but of all English cities under the operation of the English Municipal Code.

The fundamental principles of democracy have been applied to the solution of the problem of

The English Municipal System

city government with greater thoroughness in England than in any other country. The prevailing local public opinion on questions of local policy finds its expression in the Council, which is clothed with all the local governmental powers possessed by the city and whose members are responsible to the local electorate for the exercise of those powers.

The central government in England has found it entirely possible to secure from the cities due recognition of its superior authority in proper cases, and at the same time to preserve their character as local self-governing communities. The problem has been solved by the simple device of exercising the control of the central government through administrative instead of political agencies. In legal theory the Parliament in England has even more complete authority over cities than has the State Legislature in the United States.[1] There is not a section of the Municipal Code which Parliament may not alter to suit its own views. And there is no grant of power to a city which Parliament may not withdraw or modify. The English cities, in legal theory, are even more liable to the evils of "special legislation" than are the cities of the United States.[1] But in England central administrative boards have been established with general jurisdiction over all matters as to which the central authority of the

[1] No written constitution restricts the activity of Parliament.

state over the locality is to be exercised; and, where parliamentary action is necessary, it follows the lines laid down by these non-political administrative boards, whose expert and disinterested advice is frankly admitted to furnish much better and safer guidance for the determination of this class of questions than the opinions of members of Parliament who have been elected because of their views on national political issues.

Here are some contrasting examples of the methods of exercising the authority of the state over cities in England and in the United States: In both countries it is an integral part of the state policy that the power of a city to incur debt should be limited. In the United States, this is accomplished by provisions in the state constitution or by statutes restricting the debt-incurring power of the city, usually to a definite percentage of the assessed valuation of taxable property within the city limits. New York City, for instance, found it impossible, because of such a constitutional restriction, to make suitable provision for the additional water supply demanded by its rapidly growing needs without first securing an amendment to the state constitution. This requires, in New York, favorable action by two successive legislatures and a subsequent submission to the voters of the entire state for approval or rejection. Yet the experience of the city had demonstrated that its revenues from the users of water had always been more than sufficient to pay principal and income of all bonds issued for a water supply. The necessary constitutional amendment was finally secured; but only at the end of a long and costly campaign lasting for years and beset with difficulties,— the city in the meantime barely escaping the disaster of having its water supply pass under the control of a private monopoly.

In England, no constitutional restriction or act of Parliament would stand in the way. The city authorities would have submitted the project for a water supply to an administrative board (the Local Government Board) representing the central authority of the state. This board, after due public investigation, including, when desirable, the taking of testimony, and after weighing all the reasons presented for and against the project, would have rendered its decision. If an act of Parliament had been needed to carry its decision into effect the act would have been passed as a matter of course. The proceedings would have been prompt and the fairness of the decision unquestioned. In this way, many English cities have obtained their magnificent water-works.

Nor does the difference end here. The bonds issued by a city in the United States to acquire the property needed and to build and equip the water system are regulated as to their term, their sinking fund, their rate of interest, and in all other essential particulars by a rigid statute.

The special conditions of the undertaking, physical and financial, are allowed to have no influence. In England, as a rule, some central administrative board would, in connection with the local authorities, go into these with careful detail, would decide the amount to be raised, the period within which the bonds must be paid, and how the money for their repayment should be raised. The English methods are assimilated as closely as possible to those of intelligent private financiers.[1]

Or suppose that a city wishes to undertake some new function and for this purpose needs the grant by the state of additional power, in order, for instance, to manufacture and supply gas, or to own and control its street railways. In the United States, the city would have to apply to the state legislature for the grant of power, and the question whether the city should or should not undertake this new function and the conditions under which it should be allowed to do so, if at all, would become at once matters of partisan political strife. In England the ordinary course would be for the city to apply to a central administrative board (the Board of Trade), which would make a thorough and impartial investigation. The financial resources of the city would be ascertained, the locality would

[1] The details may be conveniently found in the article on "Loans" in the *Encyclopedia of Local Government Law* (6 vols., London, 1906–1908).

be visited by one of the board's officers and an opportunity given for all who desired it to be heard. There would be complete publicity at every stage and every detail would be examined with care. If the final result should be favorable to the city's application, the central administrative board, in the cases in which it did not have already sufficient authority to act, would itself prepare the appropriate bill and place it before Parliament, which would ordinarily approve the action of the central board as a matter of course.[1] The English plan insures the best expert advice and service and, what is even more important, practically eliminates politics from the supervision of local affairs by the central government.

The records of these central administrative boards and the long service of their trained assistants make available for each city the experience of all the cities. This is not only of the greatest value in reaching a wise decision, but avoids the risk of having the grant of power to the city embodied in a bill containing ambiguous or contradictory phrases which may afterwards give rise to disputes and litigation.

[1] If the board disapproves the application, the city may and occasionally does apply to Parliament directly, but favorable action by Parliament against the opposition of a central administrative board is very rare.

CHAPTER III

THE DOMINATION OF CITIES BY STATE LEGISLATURES IN THE UNITED STATES

IN theory of law, a city in the United States is a corporation, the creature of the state legislature. It has only powers enumerated by the legislature. It has no powers not enumerated in legislative grants. The legislature gives and the legislature takes away. The only restrictions upon the absolute dominion of the legislature over the city, apart from public opinion, are such as may be in the state constitution. The authoritative control of the city's public affairs is not in its citizens, but in the legislature. The city controls its own affairs only by suffrance of the legislature. The real seat of authority is not in the city, but in the state legislature. The legal validity of an act by the city, *e.g.* issuing its bonds, contracting for water-works, for a sewer or a pavement, regulating the use of its streets, is not determined by the will or expressed desires of its citizens, but by the will of the legislature as set forth in some statute. The city is not merely the creature of the legislative will, it may be and often is the helpless victim of legislative caprice.

In the exercise of the powers granted it, a city must not only keep strictly within the limits set by the state legislature, but it can follow only such administrative methods as the legislature prescribes. The only will permitted it is a mere reflex of the legislative pleasure. The legislature may regulate down to the minutest detail the methods and personnel of its administration. This street may have a railroad, that one may not; this street shall be thirty feet wide, this paved with asphalt, that with cobbles; this head of a city department be elected, that appointed; this city official have a term of three years, that one year, another an indefinite term.

A city is created by the state legislature with only such governmental powers as the legislature chooses to confer, and it must exercise its powers only in such manner and through such agencies as the legislature prescribes. Is a new power necessary or desirable, or a change wished in the methods by which it is permitted to exercise any of its powers? The state legislature and the state legislature alone can grant the new power or make the change of method.

The economic development of the country has been constantly calling an increasing number of new cities into existence and constantly enlarging the area and the population of cities already established and consequently the field of their activities. This irresistible tendency of modern industrial civilization to mass population at trade and manufacturing centres, combined with the legal subordination of the city to the central authority of the state legislature, has furnished almost boundless opportunity for misdirected legislative energy. The rural district has become a town; the town, a small city; the small city, a large one; the large city, a metropolis, all with startling rapidity. At each stage of growth the need of exercising new governmental activities has been felt in order to satisfy the local wants, and the state legislature has been called upon to confer the requisite power or to act directly through boards and commissions of its own appointment. At each stage also the administration of the general laws of the state within the city's limits and the satisfaction of the local needs have demanded increasing attention, more administrative officials, and changes of administrative plan in adaptation to the new conditions. The state legislature has been called upon to devise and control this administrative development. This process has been going on for more than half a century and is still going on before our eyes to-day. Both the process itself and the results of it may be characterized as an attempt by the state legislature to conduct the municipal government.

The helpless legal position of the city and its need of frequent application to the state legislature as the real source of power had been so continuously urgent that, until near the close of the nineteenth century, local self-government in the United States scarcely existed, either in the sense of direct management of its local interests by the city's own citizens without outside interference, or in the sense of the administration of its local scheme of government. Our people had become so accustomed to this absolute dependence upon the state legislature that there was very little genuine local public spirit. The constant resort[1] to and interference by the legislature had

[1] There has been a vast amount of legislation enacted at the request of members of the state legislature coming from the city affected or of private citizens residing there. This has been sometimes urged as showing that the city secures from the legislature the kind of local government which its citizens desire, and that local misrule has been in large measure due to too much deference by the state legislature to the wishes of the locality.

This line of reasoning assumes that such legislation was in response to a request from the whole community, when in fact it was enacted to gratify the wishes of a few, often a very few, of its members. It also loses sight of the fact that there was and could be no effective responsibility to the people of the city for enacting the legislation. Responsibility for it is diffused among legislators coming from every part of the state, and such of them as come from the city affected are not elected by the city at large but by districts, usually "safe" districts.

Legislation affecting all the people of a city enacted at the instance of only some of them is at best a perilous practice. The city is not responsible for it, however earnestly some members of the community may have desired or promoted it. It has been one of the favorite methods of exploiting our cities for personal and partisan political ends.

grown to seem perfectly natural and, as it were, inevitable in the conduct of municipal government. The cities were governed from without, not from within; such governmental powers as they might have were exercised not through methods and agencies selected by themselves but those established by outside authority. They were not self-governing communities, free to apply their own remedies to their own ills and to learn by experience how to work out an administration adapted to their local needs.[1]

Familiar as are these facts and elementary as are the legal propositions that have been stated, their tremendous consequences in American municipal history cannot be exaggerated. They have constituted one of the fundamental reasons for the corruption of legislatures, for the mismanagement of our cities, and for the lack of municipal patriotism. There has been no way to prevent or to punish the meddling by the legislature with the local policy and administration of a city government. The absolute dominion of the state legislatures over our cities has made the local voter feel helpless and hopeless and has stifled local patriotism. The exercise of power without accountability to those subject to its exercise is a gross violation of a self-evident principle of sound politics. The state legislature could make and unmake at will the

[1] See Goodnow's *Municipal Home Rule*, N. Y., 1903.

structural plan of city government; it could organize, reorganize and disorganize local methods of administration; make the positions, many times more numerous in the public service of the city than of the state, the partisan spoils of the political party which for the time being might be in the ascendant, not in the city but in the state legislature. What wonder that such power, coupled with the temptation to use it for party advantage and with no enforceable responsiblity to the citizens of the city affected, has led to the greatest abuses?

Except, however, that our senses had been dulled by long use to the usurpation by state legislatures of the functions of local government, such a legislative abuse of power would have been impossible. Even now many residents of our older states find it very difficult to conceive of a city as a self-governing community unhindered and unhelped by the state legislature. But the preposterous and utterly impracticable character of the effort to conduct local government by a state legislature will become at once apparent if we will imagine state lines to be erased and the national legislature at Washington attempting to decide the policy and order the administration of every city in the Union, from the small urban centres having but a few thousand inhabitants to the great metropolitan cities of Chicago and New York with a population mounting into the millions. Were the Congress constantly intermeddling with the local policy and internal administration of Boston and San Francisco, Chicago and New Orleans, Philadelphia and St. Louis, New York and Omaha and the other cities of the country large and small, the absurdity and iniquity of such a course would be plain to every one. It violates the most cherished principle of free government. The very idea of it is repulsive. We instinctively revolt at it and are quick to see that it is foreign to the spirit of our institutions, that local self-government is necessary to their successful or long continuance. Yet there is no essential difference in principle between the case supposed and the actual course that has been followed in Pennsylvania, for example, in New York, in Ohio, and in many other states, whose legislatures have constantly intermeddled with the local policy and internal administration of their numerous cities, large and small. Such an abuse of power would be monstrous and repellent to every self-respecting citizen of an English city. It would be difficult for him to grasp even the idea of its possibility. In a broad general sense it may be said that the English city is self-governing, while the city in the United States is state-governed. The citizens of Birmingham govern Birmingham, the legislature of Pennsylvania governs Pittsburg.

A really self-governing city is a school in civic patriotism; the city in the United States, with the constantly uninvited intervention by the legislature in its local governmental affairs, is destructive of the spirit of true democracy and is an example of cumbrous, expensive, and inefficient administration.

CHAPTER IV

CITY GOVERNMENT IN ENGLAND AND THE UNITED STATES CONTRASTED

FROM the landing of the original settlers in Jamestown and Plymouth in the early part of the seventeenth century till the middle of the nineteenth century the industrial and economic conditions in what is now the United States were not favorable to the creation of cities. Rapidly as the population increased, especially after the beginning of the nineteenth century, the country was but sparsely occupied. There was always an immense expanse of unused territory and the tendency was rather to scatter than to concentrate the habitations of the people. The population was mainly rural and the prevailing occupation was agricultural. There were many villages and small towns, but the roads were poor, the means of transportation primitive, and manufactures were carried on mainly by water-power in small isolated establishments. Even as late as the year 1850, except at a few harbors on the Atlantic seaboard and in one or two favorable situations on the banks of large rivers, the United States had almost no cities and these were rather overgrown towns than cities in the sense in which we now understand the word. The population in them was not closely compacted and the problems of city administration which have since attained such magnitude either did not exist at all or existed only in rudimentary form.[1]

During the next three decades the industrial and economic conditions in the United States changed completely. By the year 1880, the forces driving the people cityward were in full swing and cities were multiplying in numbers and growing in population with a rapidity that could not fail to attract the attention of even careless observers.

It was about 1850 that the use of steam as a source of power began to be a potent factor in the economic development of the United States and that the use of the telegraph as a means of intercommunication began. By the year 1880 the railroads had already spanned the continent and had provided for mail service, travel, and traffic a multitude of highways enormously superior in speed, in comfort, and in capacity to even the best of turnpike roads and stage coaches;

[1] In 1800, there were in the United States but six cities or towns having as many as 8,000 inhabitants. Their combined population was 210,873. Philadelphia led with 69,403; New York (county) followed with 60,489. In 1850 there were but six cities with a population in excess of 100,000 and but twenty-four having more than 20,000.

and a network of telegraph wires was rapidly spreading over the country. The economic state of 1880 was entirely new and wholly different from the economic state of 1850. The political state had changed but little; its equipment and methods, however well suited they may have been to the conditions prevailing in 1850, were altogether inadequate to meet the needs of 1880. This was true of the national government but especially of city government.

It was not until during the period from 1880 to 1890 that any considerable number of persons in the United States began to think of city government as a grave or vital matter. This was due not alone to the fact already pointed out that prior to 1850 there were almost no cities and therefore, of course, no city problem; but to the fact that the conflict between slavery and freedom had already in 1850 divided the country into two hostile camps. The economic and industrial changes that were redistributing the population and concentrating it in urban centres took place during the very period when men's minds, so far as political questions were concerned, were wholly occupied by this absorbing conflict, which culminated in years of civil war and engendered a fierce and even bigoted partisanship that prevented until the coming of another generation any prolonged and fruitful consideration of the newer problems or even an effective appreciation that there were new political problems of serious importance.

Thus it came about that when we were finally compelled by force of circumstances to begin to pay attention in the United States to city administration, we were singularly helpless. We had never given serious attention to the subject. The cities had come upon us unawares. They had been considered as merely subordinate civil divisions of the state, and the public affairs of cities, like all matters in the sphere of politics, had been treated as mere incidents of the partisan struggle for control of the national government. City government, as a problem requiring serious thought or as, in any proper sense, a problem at all, had not occurred to us. That city government was a real government, having vital need of a governmental policy of its own to be determined without any reference to the issues of national politics, was a proposition that even so recently as 1880 elicited good-natured contempt if not open derision.

We had had very brief experience with cities, our city governments were notoriously inefficient and often very corrupt, and our prejudice against the value to us of any foreign political practice, except as something to be avoided, was so strong that the long and informing municipal experience of European countries in dealing with the same problems was a sealed book. We not only had no traditions of correct administration based upon sound principles in any department of city government, but the spoils virus had been spread by the intense partisanship of our politics since Jackson's time until it had permeated and demoralized every branch of the public service, local as well as national; yet the efficient and economical performance of at least nine tenths of the functions of city government was impossible so long as there prevailed the doctrine that "to the victors belong the spoils."

The rapidly increasing needs of the growing cities had demanded continually the exercise of new governmental powers, and the constant interference by the state legislature in matters of local concern was inevitable so long as the city government was treated as a municipal corporation in strict subordination to the state legislature and possessing no powers save those which the legislative will conferred. The demoralizing results were patent to all, yet no escape seemed possible without destroying the just supremacy of the state as the central authority. This meant a chaos of special charters and special laws and the subjection of the governmental scheme of every municipality to frequent and fundamental change. It was almost literally true that each city's government was but the expression of whatever view seemed to give advantage for the time being to that political party which the shifting currents of national politics had placed in temporary control of the state legislature.

Such was the municipal situation in the United States in or about the year 1880. It was in marked contrast with the municipal situation in England, where the Municipal Corporations Act of 1835 and subsequent legislation of the same beneficent character had overcome even worse evils than those which were now besetting and demoralizing the cities in the United States and had produced a simple and stable municipal system under which, by methods well suited to the political habits of the English people, the English city had become an example of successful local self-government without disturbing or conflicting with the superior authority of the central government.

In England, to be sure, as in the United States, the municipality was, in legal theory, a corporation deriving its powers from the central legislature, but the powers were not granted, then taken away. On the contrary, if any change was made, the powers already given were enlarged or new powers were added. The municipality was, in practice, treated not as a subordinate corporation but as a local government, and the aim was to clothe it with such governmental powers as would enable it to satisfy the growing needs of the locality governed. Further, it was regarded in England as essential to a successful local government that it should be conducted according to a *local* policy, not according to a *national* or *imperial* policy. The election of the city officers charged with the duty of carrying out the local policy was made a *local* election, separate from the elections in which the attention of the voters was fixed upon questions of national policy and upon the choice of public officers charged with the duty of carrying out a national policy. In the United States, on the other hand, the municipality, in practice, was treated as a corporation temporarily clothed with only such powers as the central legislature might grant; and in so far as the municipality was a government, the policy which controlled its conduct was subordinated to the interests and the superior claims of the national political parties. The elections of city officers were but a part of the campaigns waged by the national political parties, or of state campaigns which were themselves waged upon national political issues.

In England, the fact that the municipality was a corporation deriving its life and powers from Parliament was treated as affording the opportunity to grant it the powers necessary to perform the functions of a genuine local government; while, in the United States, the fact that the municipality was a corporation was treated as the opportunity to withhold, give, alter, or withdraw powers, not in the interest of the locality, but for the temporary partisan advantage of the national political party which happened to control the legislature.

In England, the form of the city government was stable and simple; in the United States, it was subject to frequent change and was most

Contrast with English System

complex. This was because in practice a sharp and clear distinction was drawn in England between the policy determining and administrative functions of a city government, while no such distinction was made in the United States. A few brief and easily intelligible provisions in the Municipal Corporations Act had sufficed, since its enactment in 1835, to establish the political framework of government for every English city except London. There had been no changes whatever in the ground plan and no changes of any sort except in two or three minor details. In 1880, there were nearly three hundred English cities successfully conducting their governments under the plan which had been devised in 1835—and the same plan is in successful operation to-day. The plan was simplicity itself. The exercise of all the powers of the municipal corporation is committed to a board varying in membership from nine to seventy-two (or in a few cases more) according to the population of the city. The municipal electorate, at a public election held exclusively for the purpose, elect by direct vote three fourths of this board (called the Council) and the elected members choose the remaining one fourth. The former are called councillors, the latter aldermen. The aldermen have a six-year term and are chosen one half each third year. Councillors have a three-year term, one third retiring annually. Usually the city is divided into wards each of which elects every year one councillor. A member of the Council may have his residence anywhere within fifteen miles of the city limits. This is all there is to the political structure of the government of an English city and Parliament having once established it has left it alone. No exigency of imperial politics has affected it in the least.

The municipal voter in England is not only able to confine his attention to purely local issues, but he is not confused by being compelled to ascertain the records and qualifications of a long list of candidates for a large number of local public offices. The English city has practically but one elective public officer, the councillor. All others are appointees of the Council. All responsibility for the conduct of the local government is thus concentrated in the Council, one third of whose elected members come directly before the people each year to give an account of their stewardship. The record and the views of each candidate as to the local public policy are then submitted to the voters and each voter has opportunity in the simplest and most direct way to express and enforce his approval or disapproval.

The simple form of political structure prescribed for the English city not only does not interfere with but actually fosters the conduct of the local government according to local public opinion, and Parliament has left each city absolutely free to develop in its own way and according to its own notions its administrative organization. The council of each city may establish any administrative system that it deems wise and may alter it at pleasure. Thus, while the political framework of the English city government is rigid and substantially the same for every city, the administrative organization of each city is what its Council has established. It is the City Council, not Parliament that decides how the work of city administration shall be divided, what departments and bureaus there shall be, how these shall be manned and how officered, and what compensation shall be paid to the city's civil servants. Each city has an administrative equipment developed by a local board each of whose members is directly responsible for success or failure to the municipal electorate and is at all times amenable to local criticism. The practical results have been that the English municipal civil service has been kept free of both national and local politics. The political opinion of a city employé has no influence upon his tenure of office; he holds his position during efficiency and good behavior— unless he is promoted to a higher one. The city civil service, especially in the higher positions requiring expert knowledge, furnishes attractive and permanent careers for men of marked ability.

In brief, the English city, viewed in its political aspect, has a stable and simple government which the municipal voter cannot escape understanding and in the conduct of which he has a direct and effective influence; while on its administrative side the English city is equipped with a civil service in which there is not a member whose opinions on any divisive political issue have anything to do with his tenure of office.

In the United States, on the other hand, the political structure of each city government and its administrative organization have been the unstable and complicated product of state legislative activity, very often partisan in its character. The expression "each city government" is used advisedly, for the so-called "charter" of each city has been, as a rule, an accumulation of unrelated state statutes enacted from time to time with the special purpose of affecting the government of that particular city. The number of bills introduced at every legislative session for this purpose in the older states where there are many cities has been enormous, and the quantity of such special legislation that has been actually enacted has long been recognized as appalling. The administrative service of a city has been regarded as an integral part of the management of partisan politics and has been organized and reorganized with a view to partisan advantage by successive legislatures. The city, instead of having a local government conducted according to local public opinion has been treated as a subject province having now this, now that, government superimposed by an outside sovereign. Local civic spirit has been stifled.

Let the reader examine any of the city governments in the United States in 1880. He will find it the abject slave of legislative caprice; and its structural framework on both its political and its administrative side he must glean from state statutes. The legislative mind has failed to recognize any distinction between the political (or policy-determining) functions of a municipal corporation, considered as a local government, and its purely administrative functions, which must be performed whatever political policy is decided upon. To the legislative mind, in the United States, a municipal corporation was primarily and essentially a political corporation whose affairs were to be conducted in subordination to its political master—the party in control of the state legislature. It has made elective, without discrimination, purely administrative officers—such as the law officer of a city or the members of a park board—the efficient performance of whose duties depends not at all upon their opinions upon any issue which divides men into political parties, and city officers—such as aldermen—who should be chosen because of their opinions on questions of purely local political policy; and it has clothed appointive administrative officers—such as members of a health board — with legislative powers. The product of these operations of the legislative mind has been a city government, especially if it is the government of a large and important city, often very perplexing to understand. Any one who attempted really to understand it needed to be exceptionally resolute, persistent, and expert to find his way through the confused and confusing tangle of statutory provisions which held the city in their grip. But any one of ordinary intelligence would have found it an easy matter to ask and to answer correctly a number of searching questions:

Has the municipal corporation the powers requisite to perform the governmental functions which the best interests or even the pressing needs of the locality demand?

No. The legislature has granted to it only a part of these powers.

Does the municipal corporation, like other corporations, exercise such corporate powers as have been granted to it through a board of directors elected by and accountable to the members of the corporation, *i.e.* the city's voters?

No. There is no centering of responsibility, as in an ordinary corporation, for the exercise of the corporate powers, and no way of enforcing accountability to the members of the corporation for the official conduct of those entrusted with their exercise. In practice, the corporate powers and the responsibility for their exercise are distributed among a large number of officers, some elective, some appointive, with overlapping

Contrast with English System

terms of varying length, fixed by the state legislature. Their salaries are also fixed and their official duties minutely detailed by the state legislature. Practically every one of these officials, whether elective or appointive, is irremovable during his term. If he holds appointive office, his appointment was the result of a compromise or bargain between distinct appointing powers, neither of which could have made the appointment if acting alone. Some of the appointed officials are named directly by the legislature.

How is responsibility for the exercise of the corporate powers fixed?

It is not fixed and cannot be fixed amid the confusion that has just been referred to, though not by any means adequately described.

How are the elective city offices filled?

At elections when there are often elected at the same time such other public officers as members of congress, members of both houses of the state legislature, the governor and all other elective state officials, the sheriff, county clerk, and other county officials, members of the state and of the local judiciary, mayor, aldermen, park boards, water commissioners, library trustees, and numerous other elective officers and perhaps presidential electors as well.

How is it possible under these circumstances for the voter to consider city questions with any care and to cast his ballot according to his views on municipal issues?

It is impossible and it is not expected of him. The campaign before election is usually conducted on national issues and the attention of the voter is fully occupied with national political questions. Besides, he knows that it would be of little avail for him to pay attention to purely municipal matters, for the state legislature is the real governing body of his city.

Have then the city's voters, the members of the municipal corporation, no practicable and effective way of determining the policy according to which the corporation shall exercise such powers as it has?

No. The citizen of the city must submit to whatever local policy the state legislature, a partisan political body elected by the general electorate of the entire state, may impose.

But even if the city's voters have no effective way of determining the local policy, have they not through the popular elections an effective method of enforcing responsibility for the official conduct of the city's public officers?

No. There are so many officers to be elected; their official powers and duties are so widely varied; responsibility for the conduct of public affairs is so divided and dissipated; there are so many checks and counter-checks; and there are frequently also, in addition to city officers, so many county, state, or national officers to be voted for, that the citizen is helpless in the maze.

But if the electorate of the city has no practicable and effective method of holding the city's public officers accountable, in what sense can the city be regarded as a self-governing community?

In no sense. It is not a self-governing community. The government of the city is imposed upon it by outside authority neither responsible nor responsive to the electorate of the city. The city is a subject province and its affairs are conducted according to the will of its sovereign, the state legislature.

But this is not democracy?

Of course it is not. It lacks all the essential attributes of democracy. The failure of city government in the United States is not a failure of democracy.

CHAPTER V

INFLUENCE UPON CITY GOVERNMENT IN THE UNITED STATES OF THE POLITICAL DOCTRINES OF "CHECKS AND BALANCES" AND "PUBLIC OFFICES WITH SHORT TERMS"

PROPERLY understood, the movement for a city government selected by and accountable to the people of the city is a phase of the struggle for a government responsible and responsive to the people governed, which has been a chief factor in the political development of the English-speaking folk; and for more than a century, both in England and in the United States, the struggle of the people to have a direct voice and controlling influence in the conduct of public affairs has been the strongest and most persistent force in the politics of both countries. The conception of government as an authority imposed upon the people from without, and therefore to be watched and guarded against, has been more and more replaced by the conception of government as an authority created by the people themselves, accountable to them, and charged with the duty of caring

Influence of Political Doctrines 51

for the common interest. In England, where the barrier of a written constitution has not been interposed, this democratic ideal has been in some respects more nearly realized in practice than in this country. This is especially true of the government of English cities, where there has been no monarchical tradition to interfere with the democratic development.

In the United States the onward movement of democracy has been checked to a certain extent and its course somewhat deflected by the rigid barriers of written constitutions. But there could be no more convincing proof of the innate strength and persistent energy of the movement toward democracy than the futility of carefully worked out provisions placed in the federal constitution to safeguard government from the direct influence of the people.

The framers of the constitution took especial pains to devise a scheme of government that should give no opportunity for the rise of political parties or the display of political partisanship. Yet the people have been greatly aided in their efforts to have direct influence in the conduct of public affairs through competition for popular support by the political parties which were soon organized to bring about concert of action between the different departments among which the governmental powers had been distributed. In each state, the legal qualifications for electors of members of the House of Representatives—

the only department of the central government whose members could be chosen by direct popular vote—were to be those requisite for electors of the more numerous branch of the state legislature. Originally only a small fraction of the people possessed these qualifications, but the desire of the contending political parties to increase the number of their voting adherents had before the Civil War enlarged this limited electorate in state after state until practically every free white male citizen twenty-one years of age not convicted of crime was a qualified voter; and the Electoral College designed by the constitution to be a small specially selected body of the wisest and most public-spirited men who, uninfluenced by popular clamor, should choose the President, had become a merely formal register of the votes cast in an election in which practically the entire free male adult population of the country were besought to take part. In more recent times the constitutional requirement that the state legislatures should appoint the senators has been both met and evaded in a constantly increasing number of states by converting the legislatures into similar formal registers of the previously expressed preferences of the people.

The personal registration laws in many of our states, the laws regulating the casting and counting of the votes at elections, the laws establishing a secret ballot, the almost numberless statutes in recent years to liberalize the methods of nomination to public office, the civil service reform laws and rules already enacted, and the widespread movement to secure the passage of others in order to remove the spoils virus from the administrative activities of government, whether national, state or city, the efforts now making to control the so-called public service corporations in the public interest—and many other illustrations might be given—have all had a common source and inspiration, the determination of the people that the government shall be the expression of their will.

No one can understand the political history of the United States who does not recognize as the most persistent and potent factor in our political development this determination of the people to have a direct and controlling influence in the government; and their struggle to make those charged with its conduct responsible and responsive to them has never ceased. Provided progress towards this democratic goal was not in fact prevented or unduly impeded, they have paid little heed to provisions in constitution or statute or charter forbidding the progress. On the other hand, they have been eager for new laws and for amendments to old laws which promised to aid in their struggle for responsible government. If one would really understand the reason for many of the experiments that have been tried not merely in the field of government generally, but in the more limited field of city government, he must never forget that though the people have been often misled, have been frequently misinformed, and have made many mistakes, they have never abated in their determination to achieve the complete triumph in nation, state, and city of the representative principle—the rule of the people through agents and agencies chosen by the people.

Among such mistakes must be numbered, in tracing the history of our municipal development, the application to city government of the doctrines that governmental power should be so divided and distributed among those entrusted with its exercise that their several activities should serve as mutual checks and balances, and that to insure due accountability for official conduct public office should be held for a short term. No articles of their political faith were more firmly held by our forefathers.

That public officers should be required at frequent intervals to give an account of their stewardship to their fellow-citizens seemed an ideal way of preserving and enforcing responsibility and there soon began a strong movement to make more of the public offices elective. There was as yet no conscious appreciation of any important distinction between the functions of political and of purely administrative officers. Both were public officers, both were doing public work as servants of the people, and both, therefore, should be the direct choice of the

Influence of Political Doctrines 55

people and thus be directly accountable to the people for their official conduct. That increasing the number of elective officers, so far from tending to create a government responsible to the people, would produce precisely the opposite effect was not contemplated. There was not even a thought of such a result. In the states, governors and legislators were already elective; the members of the state judiciary, the attorney-general and purely clerical officers, such as secretary of state, comptroller, treasurer, surveyor, were made elective as well. In like manner, county judges, county prosecutors, and county administrative officers such as sheriffs and county clerks were made elective; and in cities the elective offices became a legion as population grew and the administrative activities of a city government increased. Elections were in some states held at the same time for all these offices, state, county and city, and often for national offices as well. The voter, confused by the multitude of candidates, found intelligent exercise of the franchise impossible. The scheme of elective offices with short terms, which was to be an ideal method of fixing and enforcing responsibility, proved, on the contrary, to be a perfect device to make it impossible either to fix or enforce responsibility. No resident of any of our older cities who voted at his last city election will doubt this if he will go over the list of offices and of candidates then presented for his consideration and endeavor to name the offices with whose duties and powers he was really familiar and the candidates of whose qualifications he had either personal knowledge or a knowledge that he felt was the result of sufficient inquiry to make him willing to put them in positions of trust in his own employment.

Because government was conceived by our forefathers as an outside authority set over the people, it was deemed the height of political wisdom to split the government into separate parts and to apportion power among these, thus creating a system of checks and balances. This theory of government found emphatic expression in the federal constitution. Its soundness and universal applicability were long considered political axioms and the doctrine was applied as a matter of course to city government as cities began to appear in the United States. But this division of power necessarily carried with it a division of responsibility, and when the division was carried still further by the multiplication of short-term elective city offices, very many of them purely administrative, it made impossible a city government responsible and responsive to the will of the citizens. In the division of governmental power and the multiplication of elective offices, responsibility to the people for official conduct was dissipated and it became a physical impossibility to investigate and pass upon the merits of a multitude of candidates for a multitude of offices. With such obstacles to overcome it is no wonder that the progress of our cities to the status of self-governing communities was very slow as compared with the English cities in which neither the check and balance system nor numerous elective offices hindered the steady evolution and intelligent application of the representative principle to municipal government.

Obviously the remedy needed both in state and city was to diminish the number of elective offices, to clothe elective public officials with greater power, to make all purely administrative offices appointive and to fill them in accordance with the merit system. Theoretically, this remedy could easily be applied to city government, for the charters of cities are merely statutes which the legislature may alter at will; and there have been notable efforts and considerable progress during the last twenty-five years in the simplification of city charters, though the number of elective offices in most of our cities is still disastrously large. But the enormous difficulty of making changes in written constitutions has in the case of national and state elective office compelled resort to another method which has exerted an influence upon the character of the changes made in many city charters so powerful that it deserves examination. Prevented by the unchangeable terms of a written constitution from eliminating the confusion by diminishing the number of elective offices among which power was divided, the American voter was yet by no means at the end of his resources. The complete transformation of presidential electors into registers of the people's will has already been noted, and the similar transformation of the state legislators into senatorial electors has been going on before our eyes. In like manner, without the alteration of a syllable in the national or state constitutions, the people have been finding another way to give effect to their desire for government responsible to them.

Nothing written in constitutions could prevent the inevitable attempt by every public officer to exalt his own, even at the expense of other offices, or the success of the attempt, if it secured general popular approval. The President of the United States and the governor of a state are necessarily the most conspicuous of the officers elected by the people. They can, if they choose, represent more directly and more effectively the wishes of a far larger constituency than any of their official colleagues. The President, when he speaks to the Congress, can claim to represent the whole country; the governor, when he speaks to the legislature, can claim to represent the whole state. He has opportunity to represent the interests of the whole people and his position gives him the strongest inducement to do so. He is one man and the Congress or the legislature is a crowd; what he does and what he says are a hundredfold more conspicuous than anything a congressman or a legislator can

Influence of Political Doctrines 59

do or say. What he does or says is always "news." His speeches will be reported verbatim and they are printed in every newspaper. He is constantly stimulated to be patriotic and public-spirited. He is not only the titular leader of his party but he may, if he chooses, be the leader of the whole people, and the people welcome his leadership and have no fear that it threatens their liberties. They feel that the courts on the one hand, and their suffrage on the other, are sufficient safeguards against that danger; that the power that such a leader exercises is conferred by their votes, that when his term ends his power will end, unless their votes continue his authority. They have seen again and again president or governor contending for the rights of the whole people against the narrower views of the Congress or the legislature; they have had frequent opportunities to applaud his vetoes of selfish or ill-considered legislative measures and have come to look upon the chief executive in the nation and the state as peculiarly representing the interests of the whole people. They believe that he has a sense of responsibility to them such as no other elected official has, and that they can enforce this responsibility more completely than in the case of other elected officials; that his fame rests upon their approval and that their condemnation can inflict a terrible punishment. They have witnessed the lasting effects of their approval and of their condemnation.

Therefore, the exaltation of the chief executive has been one of the methods through which government responsible to the people has been sought in nation, in state, and in many cities. The people are not afraid of "strong" chief executives, but are eager for them.

Intelligent application of the representative principle in the development of democratic government demands that power should be concentrated, not dispersed. Large power coupled with responsibility is not only far less dangerous than power distributed and responsibility dissipated, but it makes the government more truly representative of the people governed.

CHAPTER VI

CHANGES IN THE POPULAR ATTITUDE TOWARD CERTAIN POLITICAL DOCTRINES AND PRACTICES THAT HAVE MADE BAD CITY GOVERNMENT INEVITABLE IN THE UNITED STATES

JUST as a thoroughgoing cure of the vicious municipal conditions prevailing in England was made possible by radical improvement of the general political situation, so, in the United States, a vast amount of general political reform was a necessary preliminary to the establishment of our city governments upon a sound basis. Since the decade from 1870 to 1880, there has been a most wholesome change in our attitude toward those political doctrines and practices which made bad government inevitable, and there has been a notable advance not alone in the knowledge but in the application of sound political principles which are pre-conditions of good city government. There are thousands now, where there were tens in 1880, who have learned to appreciate the vital distinction between politics and administration, and the importance in the public interest of excluding political partisanship from a government's administrative service; and who have begun to perceive clearly the harm wrought by methods and practices which, instead of permitting city government to be conducted according to a policy determined by the local interests, make a city's elective officers the outcome of political controversies, foreign to the city's interests and having no relation to its needs.

The growing appreciation since 1880 of the distinction between politics and administration, and of the importance in the public interest of excluding political partisanship from a government's administrative service

The primary purpose of city government is to meet those ever-growing wants of the community-life which are created by the massing of population in a limited area. This is true whether the city be situated in Russia, in Belgium, or in the United States. In the very nature of things, in order to accomplish this purpose there must be, first, some policy determined upon and, secondly, when determined, this policy must be effectively carried out. There must be both a policy and an administration of the policy, or the primary purpose of city government cannot be accomplished. The determination of policy is a political matter; but, the policy once determined, the administration of the policy is a non-political, purely business matter. For example, whether a city shall build water-works directly and provide its water supply is a political question; but the faithful and competent performance of the duties of an engineer in the city's water department is a purely administrative matter requiring no opinion on his part as to the wisdom of the city's policy in regard to its water supply. Moreover, a considerable, and in the case of a city a very large, proportion of the administrative service of government must be carried on to precisely the same extent and in precisely the same manner, no matter what may be the prevailing governmental policy. It is totally unaffected by changes in governmental policy. Every official in the purely administrative public service should therefore be selected and retained by methods which exclude the consideration of his political opinions. In every country which has had the problem of city government to meet, the soundness of the distinction just pointed out between politics and administration has been demonstrated with absolute certainty. In every one of them the success or failure of their city governments on the administrative side may be measured by the extent to which the personnel of the city's civil service has consisted of officials retained for honesty, fidelity, industry, and efficiency and without reference to their partisan political opinions. The cities of Germany and England are notable illustrations. The student of the city governments of these countries finds little occasion to criticise their administrative service on the score of the inefficiency of its members or their failure faithfully to perform their duties. The function of determining public policy has in practice been kept distinct and apart from the function of actual administration. The former has been recognized as the proper sphere of politics, the latter as exclusively the sphere of business. The importance of this it is impossible to overemphasize. It is one of the chief reasons for what has been again and again held out to us as the successful solution of the problem of city government in the countries of Western Europe, widely as these may differ in the form and nature of their national governments and in their political traditions and methods.

The government of a thinly settled agricultural country has very little occasion for the exercise of administrative functions. Nor, even if the population greatly increase in numbers and wealth, is there either much need or display of activity by the administrative side of government so long as the economic conditions of the people remain simple. It was perfectly natural, therefore, and almost inevitable, that prior to the Civil War the people of the United States should pay slight heed to the methods of public administration; the more especially since the grave and exciting questions that divided the people into opposing political camps concentrated their attention upon the political functions of government. In the presence of these vital divisive political issues the non-political, purely administrative functions of government not only seemed too insignificant to attract any notice, but the intense partisanship these issues engendered made the possession or control of every public office appear a legitimate and even necessary weapon of political warfare. "To the victors belong the spoils" became an axiom in politics.

And so it came about that at the very time when, owing to changed economic conditions in the United States, the administrative activities of our government, local, state, and national, were constantly increasing, we were not only without any training in correct methods of public administration but our standards were absolutely vicious. The experience of other countries had definitely settled that, when positions in the public administrative service were mainly or largely filled by personal favorites of the appointing power, or as rewards for partisan political usefulness, the resultant corruption and inefficiency could not be confined to the strictly administrative service; and that, sooner or later, the most vital questions of governmental policy would be determined not in the public interest but by the selfish personal advantage of those who controlled the positions in the government's administrative service. The people of the United States did not wilfully disregard the experience of other countries; they simply knew nothing of it. Their ignorance did not furnish any immunity from the results of their evil practices, and it was through much bitter experience of their own that they began at last to perceive the harm inevitably wrought by patronage and spoils in the civil service.

A civil service in which the appointees are selected solely because of ascertained fitness to perform their official duties and in which the tenure of office is during efficiency and good behavior has been aptly called the merit system, and this basis of appointment and tenure is aptly called the merit principle.

When Garfield became President there was already a considerable body of intelligent public opinion insistently urging the need of a radical change for the better in the public administrative service and pointing to many examples of the demoralization and corruption resulting from a failure to adopt the merit system. The next few months furnished examples yet more flagrant. Scarcely were the inauguration ceremonies ended before the senior senator from New York precipitated an ignoble quarrel over the question whether he or the President should control the federal patronage in that state. The scandal of this controversy and the assassination of the President shortly afterwards by a disappointed office-seeker gave an impetus to the movement to better our civil service which led to the passage by Congress, in January, 1883, of a national civil service act embodying the merit principle and authorizing the President to extend the application of that principle to every appointment in the national administrative service above that of day laborer and not requiring confirmation by the Senate. Step by step under successive Presidents the number of such positions has been increased, until of the 350,000[1] employés in the civil service of the United States on June 30, 1908, 206,637[2] were appointed and held their employment under the merit system—a most conspicuous and hopeful advance.[3] The time is approaching when intelligent application of the merit principle will have expelled the debasing and unpatriotic spoils virus from the public service of the United States.

The success of the merit system in the federal civil service has had a powerful and educative influence throughout the country. In 1883, New York passed a civil service law based upon the federal statute; Massachusetts followed in 1884; Wisconsin and Illinois in 1905, Colorado in 1907, and New Jersey in 1908. There are strong movements in other states to secure the passage of civil service laws. Many individual

[1] Approximately.
[2] This is exclusive of 5,500 laborers who were under the rules but not subject to examination.
[3] The number now (December, 1908) is approximately 222,000.

cities in widely separated parts of the United States [1] and all the cities of New York and Massachusetts have placed their administrative service at least partially under the merit system. In New York the public approval of the merit principle of appointment and tenure caused the insertion in the state constitution which went into effect in January, 1895, of a clause requiring its application to all appointments and promotions in the civil service of the state and of all the civil divisions thereof including cities and villages. And there has been a progressive improvement in the enforcement of the constitutional mandate.

It is not our purpose to give a history or even a comprehensive summary of the progress and accomplishment of the civil service reform movement in the United States,[2] but enough has been already said to show how very much changed is our present attitude toward the matter of public administration. The steady growth of an intelligent appreciation of the profound distinction between the political and the non-political, the policy-determining and the purely administrative, activities of government, and of the importance in the public interest of excluding political partisanship from the public

[1] Philadelphia, Pittsburg, Chicago, Norfolk, Va., Milwaukee, Des Moines and Cedar Rapids, Ia., Denver, Seattle, Portland, San Francisco, Los Angeles and many others.
[2] See Carl R. Fish, *The Civil Service and the Patronage* (N. Y., Longmans, Green and Co., 1905).

administrative service, is an essential factor in the work of improving city government in the United States. Harmful as is the intrusion of politics into administration in the case of other governments, the resultant evils are most conspicuous in city government, for its activities, of necessity, are preponderantly administrative and it can be neither honest nor efficient without an honest and efficient civil service.

Growth of the opinion that city government should be conducted according to a local policy determined by the needs and interests of the locality

It has always been a logical absurdity, upon its face, to appeal to the national political partisanship of voters in election contests for city office, as if the public affairs of cities should be or could be governed according to any national political policy. The practical necessity is plainly apparent, if government is to reflect in its actual conduct the views of the governed, that questions of national policy, national political issues, should control in national elections and that questions of local policy, local political issues, should be uppermost in local elections. But prior to 1880, these considerations neither logically nor practically had any weight with us.

This was due in part to the fact that it is only very recently that we have begun to have any conception of city government as a real government. The expression city government has been a mere figure of speech. The city was regarded as the ward or the victim of the state legislature according as the latter was high minded and well intentioned, or was actuated by less worthy motives; but that it was a real government, a genuine political entity with the right to have a will and a policy of its own, to work out its own destiny, was a conception as yet unformed.

It was due also in part to the fact that the constitutional framework of our national government compelled from the very beginning party organization and partisanship in order to coordinate the unrelated and disparate governmental mechanism, and because the nature of the political questions which occupied the thoughts of the people for many years prior to the Civil War, and until after the reconstruction period which followed it, gave rise to an intensity of national partisanship that has no parallel except in the annals of religious warfare.

The leaders of thought in this country at the time of the American Revolution were convinced individualists in politics. They believed that to be the best government which could interfere least with individual freedom for any purpose save to administer justice. In their conception, government was something distinct and apart from the people governed; it was an outside

Changes in Popular Attitude

and superior authority, and they had a deep-seated dread lest it should prove to be an oppressive and arbitrary authority. They desired a government with as little power as was consistent with its being a government at all and with no power that it could use oppressively. The Articles of Confederation, under which a central government for the colonies, now become states, was attempted to be established after independence from Great Britain had been won, embodied these ideas. It was only the proved impotence of these articles and the imminent dissolution of the confederacy into its original parts that finally brought about the effort to establish a new central government. There were so many who even then so nearly preferred the dangers of dissolution to the risks involved in submitting to a central government with larger authority, that it was well-nigh impossible to prepare a new fundamental charter to which even so many as nine of the thirteen states would agree. There was no dispute that the new central government should have no power that it could use oppressively, but the separatist tendencies of a very considerable minority made them quick to suspect possible oppression. Concessions were constantly necessary and the Constitution of the United States which finally replaced the weak Articles of Confederation was a series of compromises.

The new central government which was at

last agreed upon had no powers not enumerated in the constitution. This was one limitation upon its authority. The government was divided into several departments, the Judiciary, a President, and the Congress, which in turn was subdivided into a Senate and a House of Representatives. The powers enumerated in the constitution were distributed and apportioned among these, some to one, some to another; while some, in order to be exercised, required the joint action of two or more departments. There were certain governmental powers which the President might exercise of his own motion; others which he could exercise only with the concurrence of the Senate; and others required the concurrence of the Congress. This was another limitation. These and many other provisions in the constitution testify to the careful precautions taken against the possibility of oppression by the new government. Moreover, the Supreme Court, when occasion demanded, passed upon the question whether the power attempted to be exercised had in fact been granted by the constitution and whether the manner of its attempted exercise was in accordance with the constitution.

If the men who framed our constitution dreaded the oppression of a strong government, their dread was no less real of a government whose policy could be influenced by impulse or passion. A government which was the direct expression of the people's will would have seemed to them dangerous. They did not believe in the political sanity of the people. A government of the people, by the people, for the people would, to their minds, have seemed neither safe nor stable. On the contrary, they desired a government so planned that its policy would always necessarily be the result of the mature deliberations of experienced and superior men. The limitations already existing upon the suffrage made a qualified electorate which was but a fraction of the general body of the people. This to their minds diminished but did not remove the danger of hasty or ill-considered action. The constitution, therefore, provided that this limited electorate should have no direct voice in the conduct of the new central government beyond electing members of the House of Representatives, who were given a term of two years; that the state legislatures should choose the senators, whose term of office was made six years; and that the President should be chosen every four years by a specially selected electoral body consisting of electors from each state appointed in such manner as its legislature might direct, the number from each state to be equal to the number of senators and representatives to which the state was entitled in the Congress.

These are some of the measures taken by the men who framed our constitution to guard the people against the oppression of a strong government and to guard the government against the unripe thought and unstable impulses of the people. The government was to be of the whole people and for the whole people, but by the best people, who were to be ascertained through a carefully devised selective process.

Among other important aims which this plan was to accomplish was the abolition of political partisanship. The public policy of the country was to be the result of the earnest but calm deliberations of the wisest and best. But the disparate, slow-moving governmental machinery with its mutually interfering parts continually checking and blocking one another, soon proved in practice to be cumbrous and unworkable without the application of some external unifying force. The government of divided powers and responsibilities established by the constitution made political parties and political partisanship a necessary co-ordinating agency to overcome the centrifugal tendencies of the constitutional plan when put into actual operation, and to make possible united and harmonious action by the different authorities among which the powers of the central government had been distributed. From the very foundation of our government, therefore, national political parties have striven to control the government and to direct its conduct according to the policies they favored.

The recognition of slavery as an institution entitled to the protection of the central government was one of the compromises contained in the constitution. This gave rise to bitter and prolonged political controversy in the issue of which both sides felt that the continuance of the Union, the very life of the nation, was at stake. The heat of the controversy was intensified by the fundamental irreconcilability of the economic interests of the contending parties and by their radically opposed social and ethical standards. While this controversy raged there was no politics but national politics and no political partisanship but national political partisanship.

No one of the present generation can form an adequate idea of the partisan heat and political bigotry of the period just before, during, and for a considerable time after the Civil War. Men were not partisans merely, they were political zealots. Their political beliefs were held with the tenacity with which honest religious bigots cling to their creeds. The man who left his party was an apostate, the man who did not belong to one of the recognized political parties was an outcast. Even as late as the year 1880, there was little perceptible abatement in the heat of blind and unreasoning partisanship, though slavery had been extirpated, the Union had been preserved, and no party threatened the life of the nation.

Gradually, however, even the embers of the old controversy have been extinguished. The great majority are still the confirmed adherents of one or other of the national political parties; but each year since 1880 has increased the number of those who act now with one, now with another party, according to the strength of the appeal its principles, its leaders, and its behavior make to their reason. The independent voter, the man who owns no fixed allegiance to any one party, is no longer a pariah. Though he is still in a minority, it is a minority that not infrequently decides elections. It is no longer certain that the vote of a state will be cast for the candidates of the same party for national and state office even in the same election; the Republican presidential electors may carry a state by a large majority and yet a Democratic governor be elected. It is no longer an unheard-of thing that the successful candidates for state offices at the same election belong to different political parties. The blind and bigoted partisanship, the heat and passion which characterized the political contests of twenty-five years ago, have been largely replaced by a marked degree of discrimination among the voters.

This is notably the case in elections to local office. The dominance of national politics in local elections has sensibly diminished. In many important and widely separated cities there are strong organizations proclaiming and endeavoring to enforce the doctrine that questions of national politics should be excluded from local campaigns. In many of our states one may retain his position as a member in good and regular standing of his national political party though he is known to act independently in local politics. In some states the national political party organizations have formally announced that their members may have entire freedom in voting for candidates for local office. It is not very unusual for the local branch of a national political party to bid for popular support of its candidates for city office upon the ground that, if elected, they will administer the office in the interest of the city rather than of the national party. We have even of late years had local elections in which no national political question has been discussed in the press or on the platform; and the growth and prosperity of newspapers which in their treatment of local public affairs are genuinely free of all national political bias are phenomenal. The constitution of New York State which went into effect on January 1, 1895, separated city elections from national elections by a whole calendar year for the avowed purpose of facilitating the conduct of city government independently of the influences of national political partisanship.

The doctrine that national politics have no proper place in the determination of local political elections is still far from general acceptance; but one has only to remember the astonishment and incredulity with which prior to 1880 he would have heard of such occurrences as these that have been mentioned taking place anywhere in the United States to appreciate the marvellous change since then in popular sentiment. The incongruity and absurdity of the intrusion of national politics into the local field, and the positive harm to the city of subordinating its local interests to the claims of national political partisanship, thereby preventing the city from having or following a local policy suited to its own needs, are now demonstrated truths both logically and practically. Their influence is widespread and it is constantly becoming wider.

CHAPTER VII

GROWTH OF THE DETERMINATION THAT THE CITY SHOULD HAVE A LOCAL GOVERNMENT RESPONSIBLE TO THE PEOPLE OF THE CITY

THE people of the United States have been coming more and more to understand that the government of our cities has been not in conformity with but in violation of the representative principle; that the bad government of our cities has been not so much by the cities themselves as by outside superimposed authority not accountable to and not chosen by the citizens of the city; that a city subject to constant ravages by the state legislature can have no local policy of its own; that a city government without power to satisfy the needs or protect the interests of the city lacks both the dignity and the authority to command the respect of its citizens or arouse the feeling of local patriotism. We have been learning the lesson that, if the cities are to be well governed, they must be self-governing. Like progress at the same rate for another twenty-five years should make our cities really self-governing communities, free to work out their own destinies.

At the beginning of the last quarter of the nineteenth century practically every city government in the United States could be generally described as follows:

It was a corporation created by statute and possessed only such governmental powers as the state legislature granted from time to time and permitted it to retain and such administrative system as the state legislature for the time being prescribed;

In its general form, a city government copied that of the national government. There was always a locally elected mayor and a legislative body, the latter consisting of one and frequently two chambers; and there were various administrative departments, police, fire, water, etc., whose heads, sometimes individuals and sometimes boards, held office for fixed terms and, when not appointed by the state, were elected by popular vote or chosen by the local legislative body or one of its chambers, sometimes upon previous nomination by the mayor;

No city had all the powers of government requisite to satisfy its local needs—many had very restricted power—but there was almost no governmental power which some city did not possess and exercise;

Elections to city, as well as to county, state,

and national office were treated as integral parts of national political campaigns.

There are multiplying evidences that the popular conception of city government has been undergoing a great and radical change. As already pointed out there has been since the decade between 1870 and 1880 a clearer and clearer appreciation by our people of the wisdom of keeping politics and administration apart in the conduct of government, and a constantly increasing perception of the grave damage to the public interests of the cities, and of the nation as well, by illogically involving questions of purely local concern in the strife of national political parties. There have also been notable efforts on the part of many of our cities to free themselves from legislative domination, to obtain grants of power adequate to care for all matters of purely local concern, to secure and enforce accountability to the city's voters for the exercise of the powers granted, and, to that end, to simplify the form of city government. A statement, even if it be only a summary one, of what has been and is being done by some of our cities to accomplish these results cannot fail to be instructive. The lines of effort and the degrees of success attained have varied in the different states, sometimes widely, as was to have been expected with a people so resourceful and inventive as ours, but this very variety brings out clearly the oneness of purpose.

The concentration of power in the mayor.

The attitude of the American people toward the executive branch of the government is in interesting and significant contrast to the dread of the executive which was so influential in determining the form of government the framers of our national constitution devised. After a century's experience of the actual operation of the constitutional checks and balances, the abuse of power that the people fear is by the legislative, not by the executive branch of the government; the executive has risen and the legislative sunk in the confidence of the people. Of the many illustrations of this, the increasing number of restrictions upon and regulations of legislative activity placed in our state constitutions, as from time to time new states are admitted to the Union or the older states adopt new constitutions, is significant. So has been the successive deprivation of the aldermen, or other local legislative body in the cities, of legislative power.

When, therefore, persistent bad government in the cities of the United States began to compel effective attention and we began to perceive that a city government irresponsible to the people of the city was one of the main causes of the low estate into which municipal administration had sunk, one of the lines of remedial effort which previous political experience commended was the enlargement of the power of the mayor, the city's chief executive. The structural plan of the government found in the usual city charter prior to 1880 was an exaggerated reproduction of the government of divided powers and responsibility in the Constitution of the United States, but there was a far more minute division of power. Such governmental powers as the city possessed were divided among various elected officials many of whom performed purely administrative duties. The mayor was a mere simulacrum of a chief executive and the powers that he could exercise of his own motion were usually of slight importance. The appointive heads, whether individuals or boards, of the city departments, were such persons as the mayor and the local legislative body or, in some cases, the local legislative body acting alone, could agree upon. These held office for fixed terms, often for a period beyond the mayor's own tenure, and could be removed by him only upon formal charges and after a trial in which the officer was regarded as an accused person entitled to counsel and often having the right of appeal to the governor or to the courts and sometimes to both. Here were checks and balances enough, and pretty nearly complete irresponsibility on the part of both the elected and the appointed officials.

It was argued that the mayor should be the chief executive of the city in fact as well as by title, that heads of the city departments should be appointed by the mayor and should be removable at his pleasure. So long as the spoils doctrine prevailed in the appointments to its civil service it was recognized that the conduct of the city's public affairs would still be wasteful and inefficient; but it was urged that, if the citizens could hold the mayor accountable for the kind and quality of the service rendered, this would be a long step toward securing a city government responsible to the people.

This argument secured a strong popular support in the city of Brooklyn (New York) and the state legislature permitted that city in a small and tentative way to test its merits by a practical application. The mayor of Brooklyn by an amendment to its charter was given power during thirty days after he took office to remove and appoint at pleasure non-elective heads of city departments. The first election under the amended charter took place in November, 1881, and aroused a general interest among the voters never witnessed in any previous election. The city was strongly Democratic on national issues, but was carried for the mayoralty candidate of the Republicans and Independents. He entered upon the duties of his office on January 1, 1882, and promptly appointed heads of each city department. The results of the experiment were so successful that the "Brooklyn Idea," as it was called, has markedly influenced charter changes in many other cities of the state,[1] and, supported and pressed by powerful public sentiment, has revolutionized the position and powers of the mayor in Brooklyn and its adjacent city of New York and in the greater city of New York of which they now are a part. The division and dissipation of responsibility among the members of a board has been replaced by making a single head accountable for the efficiency of a city department. This change also has worked well. New York City, for example, formerly had a board of police commissioners, a board of dock commissioners, and so on; it now has a police commissioner and a dock commissioner. Moreover, the tenure of office of the head of a city department is no longer a fixed term. He may retain his position under successive mayors without reappointment, but the mayor can remove him at pleasure.

Thus, in the local government of the territory

[1] "The mayors of the six largest cities in New York State, of Boston, of all cities in Indiana, and a few other cities, have now the sole and absolute power of appointing the heads of most of the municipal departments; and in the same cities, with the addition of the four largest cities in Pennsylvania, mayors have the power of removing at any time the appointed heads of departments. Under this system the executive authority and responsibility is concentrated in the mayor, except for a few officials still elected by popular vote."—Fairlie, *Essays in Municipal Administration* (New York, 1908), p. 22.

now comprised in the city of New York, a revolution has taken place since January 1, 1882. The heads of each city department are accountable to the mayor, who is responsible for their efficiency to the people who elect him as the executive head of all the departments. If the other provisions of the charter were as simple and direct, the greater city of New York would have an opportunity to furnish an admirable example of a completely self-governing community. As it is, stimulated by the changes already noted and aided by the gradual spread of the merit system in the subordinate city civil service, its government has grown better and better and there has been developed a stronger and more widespread local patriotism than was even thought possible twenty-five years ago. There has been an ever more insistent demand for more power in order to conduct its local affairs without applying to the legislature, and a constantly growing resentment at legislative interference with the exercise of local powers already granted. In this feeling the other cities of the state strongly shared, and in the state constitution which went into effect January 1, 1895, there was incorporated a provision sometimes called the "Mayor's Veto." The cities of the state are divided into three classes and every bill relating to a single city, or to less than all the cities of a class, must, after passing the legislature, be sent to the mayor of the city affected. After public notice and opportunity for a hearing, if the mayor of a first-class city (or the mayor and local legislative body of a city of the other classes) does not accept the bill within fifteen days, it must be repassed by the legislature before transmission to the governor for his action.

Safeguarding the city from the state legislature by constitutional provisions.

The meddling by the state legislature with the local affairs of cities to their great damage has led to the adoption in many of our states of constitutional provisions which endeavor to correct the evil.[1] Their terms have varied in the different constitutions, but each has sought to prevent or regulate special legislation in reference to cities. This was one of the earliest means tried to better city government. For various reasons, this method has not proved as efficacious in practice as had been hoped, but the lessons which is has taught have been of great value. In one state, Illinois, the constitutional prohibition against special legislation has been so interpreted by the courts as to be a far more successful defence against ingenious attempts to evade it than has usually been the case.

[1] A statement showing those restrictions in tabulated form (Constitutional Limitations Relating to Cities and Their Affairs) may be found in the *Annals of the American Academy* (January, 1906), p. 232.

This has led to a very interesting and highly instructive illustration of the persistent efforts the people of a city are willing to make to control its government if no outside authority can interfere. It has also furnished concrete and convincing evidence to all men that in the United States, *if no outside authority can help or hinder*, the citizens of a city will find a way to control its government.

When the citizens of Chicago began to be aroused to some consciousness of the low character of its government and sought a remedy, they pursued a course in striking contrast to that taken in other cities and undertook the reformation of the city's Council. This apparently hopeless task was successfully accomplished and Chicago's local legislature became worthy of the confidence of its citizens.

That Chicago in a few years should have so far changed the character of its Council that it became a body in whose honesty and competence the people of the city could confide is certainly a splendid achievement. But the real significance of what Chicago did, the lasting and permanent contribution it made to the betterment of municipal government in the United States, is in the circumstances and conditions under which this result was accomplished.

Chicago's government was bad, but it was not more desperately bad than the government of Philadelphia or New York City, for example.

Yet neither Philadelphia nor New York has made any improvement in its government through elevating the character of the local legislature. Little, if any, thought and no effort worth mentioning have been bestowed, in either of those cities, upon this method of bettering the conduct of local affairs. In New York, for instance, the Board of Aldermen, thoroughly discredited by the improvident and unworthy use of the powers entrusted to it, has been gradually stripped of most of the authority it formerly had and the thought and efforts of those who sought to obtain a city government responsible and accountable to the people of the city have been directed toward the enlargement of the power of the mayor. But the New York aldermen were no more thoroughly discredited and no more unworthy of trust than the councilmen of Chicago. Why then did Chicago, when it began to feel the stirrings of a civic conscience, undertake the immensely laborious and apparently hopeless task of making over its Council and persist until it accomplished what had been considered wholly impossible? *It was because there was no other way.*

In Illinois, recourse to the legislature for aid, and meddling by the legislature, were alike shut off by the state constitution. The legislature could not deprive Chicago's councilmen of their power and the people of Chicago could not successfully appeal to the legislature for any change in the structural plan of the city government.

However ill-fitted might be the charter of Chicago to the needs of the city, no change in it could be made through the aid of the legislature. Protected from legislative interference and cut off from legislative aid and subject to the restrictions of an unamendable city charter, the people of Chicago were obliged either to continue to submit to bad city government or to transform the personnel of its Council. There was no alternative.

In New York, on the other hand, the legislature of its own motion and at the suggestions of residents of the city was habitually modifying, revising, or repealing this or that provision of the huge congeries of statutes under which the city government was conducted. Nothing was final. The city government at any given time was simply one of a series of legislative experiments. The legislature was always meddling and some one claiming to represent local interests was always appealing to the legislature. The number of bills affecting the city government introduced at each session of the legislature mounted into the hundreds, and scores of them were enacted into law at every session. Under these conditions it is not surprising that the bettering of city government in New York through the elevation of the character of its aldermen was not seriously attempted nor even seriously considered. This contrast in basic conditions between New York and Chicago explains why the two cities proceeded along such different lines in their efforts to secure a local government really responsible to the people of the locality— the one by concentrating power in the mayor, the other by improving the personnel of its City Council.

That Chicago should alone among our cities have succeeded in transmuting its Council from a public menace into a competent and really representative local legislature, which can be safely entrusted with large authority, is most significant. To students of the city problem in the United States, the most instructive lesson, the supreme significance of Chicago's experience, is this: *Alone of all our great cities, Chicago's form of government was unamendable; the state legislature was obliged to leave Chicago's local government alone.*

Home-made city charters.

The people of each state, when it comes into the Union, and from time to time thereafter, elect delegates to a convention which frames a fundamental charter for the state government. When ratified by the people at a general election— occasionally without such ratification—this becomes the organic law and is controlling upon every citizen and every department and official of the state government until it is amended in like manner by the people. Why should not the people of a city as well as the people of a state have a charter of their own making and thus be able to have a government adapted to their local needs, changing it from time to time as occasion requires? Why should any outside authority impose a government upon the city? Why should the city not evolve one for itself? These perfectly natural questions have been answered in the affirmative by the people in several states.

In 1875 the state of Missouri had a constitutional convention. The delegates from St. Louis were instructed by their constituents to secure the insertion in the new state constitution of provisions which would give St. Louis the right to make its own charter and would protect the city from interference by the state legislature in the city's local affairs. The attempt was measurably successful. The new state constitution which was ratified by the people at the autumn election in 1875 provided that "any city having a population of more than 100,000[1] inhabitants may frame a charter for its own government, consistent with and subject to the constitution and laws of this state." A board of thirteen freeholders elected by the people of the city was to draft the charter, which, if subsequently ratified at the polls, should "supersede any existing charter and amendments thereof." The state constitution required that the charter

[1] St. Louis was separately provided for, but on essentially the same plan. St. Louis was the only city in Missouri at the time having more than 100,000 inhabitants.

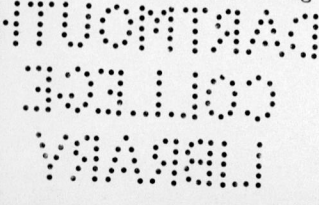

should provide for a mayor and a two-chamber council, of which at least one branch should be elected on a general ticket; prescribed the qualifications of the "freeholders" and the manner of their election; set forth how the draft of the charter should be submitted to the people of the city and how amendments to it might be made from time to time; and contained other important details of procedure as well as a number of limitations and restrictions, the result of all of which was that the city had by no means the absolute freedom that one might suppose from the general language quoted. But the contrast with its previous thraldom to the state legislature was great.

St. Louis promptly enacted a freeholders' charter, and its new government proved to be so superior to any the state legislature had previously permitted, that California adopted the same general plan for its cities having a population of more than 100,000 (that is, for San Francisco), but required that the charter, after its passage by the people of the city, should be submitted to the legislature for approval.[1] These provisions of the California constitution went into effect January 1, 1880. The submission to the legislature proved in practice to be a merely formal matter; and in 1887 the right to frame their own charters was extended to all cities having

[1] The legislature could approve or disapprove, but could not amend the proposed charter.

more than 10,000 inhabitants, and in 1890 to those having more than 3,500.

The California constitution of 1880 made such a charter supersede all "special laws" inconsistent therewith. This made trouble, and in 1892 another constitutional amendment struck out the word "special." There was still trouble, for the home-made charter provisions had to be construed in connection with other constitutional provisions, and in 1896 still another constitutional amendment was adopted, which provided in terms that such charters "*except in municipal affairs* should be subject to, and controlled by, general laws." This placed the supremacy of the city in purely local matters beyond question. This sketch of California experience gives conclusive proof of the strong desire of the people to have a government of their own making.

In 1889, the state of Washington followed the example of Missouri and California and adopted a constitutional provision giving to every city having 20,000 inhabitants considerable authority to frame its own charter. Minnesota followed in 1896, granting such authority under certain constitutional restrictions to every city without regard to its population; and in 1902, similar provisions applicable to all cities of the first and second classes[1] were incorporated in

[1] In 1908 this included all cities having a population of 2,000 or more.

the constitution of Colorado. In 1906, Oregon incorporated a home-made charter provision in its constitution. Oklahoma entered the Union with such a provision in its constitution in 1907, and Michigan's new constitution[1] (adopted November, 1908) provides a method by which the cities of that state may have very considerable freedom in the framing and amendment of their charters.

The constitutions of Missouri, California, Washington, Minnesota, Colorado, Oregon, Oklahoma, and Michigan show many differences, some of them important, in their respective provisions

[1] "The legislature shall provide by a general law for the incorporation of cities, and by a general law for the incorporation of villages. . . . Under such general laws, the electors of each city and village shall have power and authority to frame, adopt, and amend its charter, and, through its regularly constituted authority, to pass all laws and ordinances relating to its municipal concerns, subject to the constitution and general laws of the state." Art. VIII, §§ 20, 21.

"Any city or village may acquire, own, establish, and maintain, either within or without its corporate limits, parks, boulevards, cemeteries, hospitals, almshouses, and all works which involve the public health or safety." Art. VIII, § 22.

On the affirmative vote of three fifths of the electors of a city or village voting thereon at a regular or special municipal election—and upon such proposition women taxpayers having the qualifications of male electors shall be entitled to vote —any city or village may acquire, own, and operate, either within or without its corporate limits, public utilities for supplying water, light, heat, power, and transportation to the municipality and the inhabitants thereof; and may also sell and deliver water, heat, power, and light without its corporate limits to an amount not to exceed twenty-five

for city-made charters. In none of the states mentioned are the cities entirely free to have a government of their own devising,[1] but in spite of many hampering restrictions these home-made charters have been invariably superior to the state legislative products they displaced, and it is generally the case also that each successive home-made charter is an improvement on the one that preceded it. The movement for home-made charters points very clearly to one way of achieving a city government responsible and responsive to the people of the city. This does not necessarily mean that a city clothed with complete power for self-government would immediately be a well-governed city. The people must first govern themselves before they govern themselves well. They certainly cannot remedy bad government unless they have a direct and controlling voice in the conduct of government. The spread of the "Missouri Idea" is a noteworthy

per cent. of that furnished by it within the corporate limits; and may operate transportation lines without the municipality within such limits as may be prescribed by law: Provided, that the right to own or operate transportation facilities shall not extend to any city or village of less than twenty-five thousand inhabitants. Art. VIII, §§ 25, 23.

[1] The number of cities is constantly growing which prefer these "home-made" charters. To mention some of them: In Missouri, St. Louis and Kansas City have framed their own charters so far as they have been free to do so; some twenty of the cities of California, including San Francisco, Sacramento, and Los Angeles; about a score of the cities of Minnesota; Seattle, Spokane, and Everett in the state of Washington; Denver, Colorado.

indication of the growing recognition of the right of cities to have control of their local affairs without interference by the state legislature and to that end to frame their local governments themselves.

City government by a board of directors.

Texas and certain other of the states that have followed its example have been recently attempting to reach the goal of responsible local government by an adaptation of the English plan of a locally elected council which shall exercise such powers as the city has under its charter after essentially the same fashion as a board of directors[1] exercises the charter powers of a corporation.

[1] Because the members of the Galveston board were called commissioners the title " City Government by Commission" was early given to this method of city government. To Eastern ears, familiar with state-appointed commissions and commissioners to perform purely local functions, this expression is most misleading. It sometimes leads to the impression that, in so far as this " Government by Commission" is successful, it goes to prove that city government is *business*, not government, and therefore best conducted by a few business men on strictly business principles as an entirely subordinated agency of the state. On the contrary, city government according to the "Galveston Idea" is at the very opposite political pole. The elected officials it calls commissioners are closely analogous to the selectmen of the New England towns, and like them are responsible to the local electorate. The " Commission " system may also be compared to the commissioner type of county government which prevails in many states.

In 1900, Galveston, Texas, had the usual type of city government in the United States, the usual type both as to general form of government and as to quality of administration. The private business of its citizens was prosperous, but the city itself was without financial strength; its sanitary condition was poor, its streets were in bad condition, and the police did not enforce the laws. A great hurricane swept the city and left it prostrate. The city is situated on low ground and its defences from the Gulf were destroyed. The private business of its people was no longer prosperous; its bonds fell to sixty and the bankruptcy of the city and its citizens was impending. The emergency was beyond the ability of the city government, and with ruin staring them in the face its citizens had no choice but either to abandon their homes and start in business in some other place or to remain where they were and rescue Galveston. They quickly discovered that responsibility under the existing charter was divided and dissipated and that their first need was the simplification of their form of government in order to concentrate responsibility. They asked the state legislature to change the charter and vest in a small board all the legislative and executive authority of the city. The legislature made the necessary changes and the experiment began in the autumn of 1901. The governing body of the city was made a small board of five members, a mayor-president and four associates, the mayor and two of his associates appointed by the governor, the two others elected at large. The appointment by the governor was subsequently declared unconstitutional by the courts, and beginning in 1903 all the members of the board were made elective.

The city's public affairs are apportioned among four departments, and the board by majority vote assigns one of its members to the headship of each department. The mayor is general manager, but, except in certain unusual cases, which do not concern us, has no greater authority than any of his associates. His vote counts for no more than the vote of any of the others. The five directors are all chosen at the same time and for a term of two years. The election is a purely local election and takes place in May. The five original members of the board were a lawyer, a banker, a wholesale merchant, a real estate dealer, and the secretary and treasurer of a live stock company. The only change in personnel has been the selection of another wholesale merchant to succeed the lawyer, who died in 1905.

This board of five directors not only rescued the city financially—its bonds rose to a premium —but remade the city physically, brought its sanitary condition up to a high standard, and under them the city's police enforced the law. All this was accomplished with a saving of one third in the running expenses.

100   Government of American Cities

Houston, another Texan city, stimulated by the example of Galveston, secured in 1905 a charter granting it the Galveston form of government, and the charter powers of that city are exercised by a board of five directors, a mayor and four aldermen, all elected on a general ticket. In Houston four of the five men chosen as directors were well known in local politics and had held city office. The same results have been accomplished as in Galveston,— running expenses reduced, debts paid off, physical appearance of the city bettered, sanitation improved, water and other public services made efficient, law enforced. Other Texan cities have applied for and been granted similar charters, as have also the cities of Lewiston, [1] in Idaho, and Haverhill [2] and Gloucester, [3] in Massachusetts. By special acts of the state legislature, Iowa,[4] Kansas,[5] North Dakota,[6] South Dakota [7] in 1907 and Mississippi [8] in 1908 each enacted a general law under which cities may, if they choose, have charters embodying the general features of the Galveston plan.[9] The

[1] Laws of 1907, House bill No. 121.
[2] Laws of 1908, Chapter 574.
[3] Laws of 1908, Chapter 611.
[4] Laws of 1907, Chapter 48.
[5] Laws of 1907, Chapters 114, 123.
[6] Laws of 1907, Chapter 45.
[7] Laws of 1907, Chapter 86.
[8] Laws of 1908, Chapter 108.
[9] Des Moines and Cedar Rapids (Iowa), Leavenworth (Kansas), Mandan (North Dakota), Sioux Falls (South

Iowa and South Dakota laws were not content with simplifying the city charter and concentrating the responsibility for local government in the hands of a small board of directors locally elected. In order the more surely to secure direct control by the people over the local government they incorporated provisions for the initiative, the referendum, and the recall.

The Newport plan.

In the New England town a board of selectmen elected by the general body of the voters has immediate charge of the town administrative service; but the corporate powers of the town are exercised directly by the voters themselves assembled in town meeting and the selectmen are subject to the orders and resolutions there adopted. Many New England towns, even after they have grown so populous as to be properly rated as cities, have clung to this town meeting plan as on the whole securing a local government more nearly in accord with the local public opinion than any of the more elaborate plans that have been substituted in its stead when a general gathering of the voters in one meeting place has become impossible. Newport, Rhode Island, since Janu-

---

Dakota), have adopted such charters. The Des Moines plan of city government was held constitutional by the Iowa Supreme Court in Eckerson *v.* Des Moines (115 N. W. 177).

ary, 1907, has been trying an experiment [1] intended to demonstrate that the essential features of government by town meeting may be applied successfully in a city of twenty-five thousand inhabitants.

To supply the place of the ancient town meeting and to perform its functions, Newport elects a delegate council so numerous as to be really representative of the general body of the voters and yet not so numerous as to prevent its meeting together. Each of the five wards of the city has thirty-nine delegates—thirteen are elected annually for a term of three years—to a "Representative Council" of one hundred and ninety-five members who serve without pay. The council is the judge of the election of its own members, chooses its own chairman, and adopts its own rules of procedure. The records of its proceedings are public. Any voter and any taxpayer (man or woman) may attend its meetings and speak, but only members may vote. The representative council makes up the budget, levies the taxes, makes all the appropriations, fixes the salaries of the city employés, elects and removes city officials not elected by popular vote, and in general is vested with all the legislative powers possessed by the city. Any twenty-five of its members or the board of aldermen by filing a written request with the city clerk can require a meeting of the council to be held.

To supply the place and perform the functions

[1] Laws of Rhode Island, 1906, Chapter 1,392.

Local Self-Government the Goal

of the selectmen of a New England town, a mayor and five aldermen, one from each ward, are elected annually. They are paid salaries and have immediate charge of the city's administrative service subject to the orders of the council. They must attend the meetings of the council and give any information requested.

The Newport plan includes both the initiative and the referendum as to public expenditures. At the council's meeting in January, its chairman must appoint a committee of twenty-five, five from each ward, to prepare a budget for the ensuing year and submit it for the action of the council at a later meeting. This budget must be printed and sent to all taxpayers[1] at least seven days before it is acted upon. No vote or appropriation involving the expenditure of more than $10,000 becomes operative for seven days. If within this period a petition is filed signed by one hundred and fifty taxpaying voters—there must be at least ten from each ward—the proposition

[1] Under the constitution of Rhode Island only persons who paid taxes on at least $134.00 of property in the preceding year can vote for members of a city council or on a proposition to propose a tax in any city or involving the expenditure of city money. The taxpayer vote of Newport numbers approximately 3,900, the general electorate includes about 1,200 more. The city election occurs on the first Monday of December, approximately a month after the general election. Candidates for mayor are voted for by the general electorate of the city. The taxpayer vote of each ward chooses its representatives in the council. The alderman from the ward is chosen by the taxpayer vote of the entire city.

must be submitted to the general taxpaying electorate of the city for ratification. A petition signed by one hundred taxpaying voters can compel the council to act upon any proposition for the expenditure of more than $10,000, and if the council's action be adverse, three hundred taxpaying voters—there must be at least twenty from each ward—can by petition compel the proposition to be submitted to the taxpaying electorate of the city.

Nominations to the elective city offices are made by filing nomination papers at least twelve days before election. Nomination papers for a member of the council must be signed by at least thirty taxpayers of the ward; nomination for alderman by at least one hundred taxpayers of the city; for mayor by at least two hundred and fifty of the general electorate. Every nomination paper must contain the acceptance of the nomination by the candidate and the names and addresses of the nominators. No partisan political statements or emblems are permitted to appear on the nomination paper or on the election day ballots.

The government of the city has shown marked improvement during the two years since the new plan was inaugurated. Its advocates lay special stress upon its separation of the taxing and spending authority. The Newport plan is another example of the determination to find a way to compel city government to be conducted in accordance with the local public opinion. There are indications already of its serious consideration by other cities.

The Initiative, the Referendum, and the Recall as applied to the conduct of city government.

Each of these methods of enforcing the popular will takes various forms. The initiative may be described generally as a right granted by law to any group of voters, comprising at least a given proportion of the electorate, to submit and compel action upon a proposed law of its own drafting. Sometimes the submission is to the legislature, sometimes to the direct vote of the general electorate without the intervention of the legislature; sometimes, in the event of unfavorable action by the legislature upon the proposed measure, the initiative compels its subsequent submission to the voters at large at a special or general election. Under the referendum a similar group of voters may make nugatory a law enacted by the legislature unless it be ratified at a subsequent popular election. Under the recall a similar group of voters may compel an elected public officer, before his statutory term expires, to secure the approval of his official conduct by a popular vote or give way to a successor.

Some form of the initiative, the referendum, or the recall, and sometimes of all three, is already in experimental use in many cities and the number is constantly growing.[1]

The referendum as to state legislation is provided for in the constitution of Nevada,[2] and both the initiative and the referendum in the constitutions of South Dakota,[3] Utah,[4] Oregon,[5] Montana,[6] Oklahoma,[7] Maine[8] and Missouri.[9] In North Dakota, initiative and referendum amendments are pending in the state legislature. Under specific provisions of the constitutions of Oregon,[10] Oklahoma,[11] South Dakota[3] and Maine,[8] cities enjoy the rights of initiative and referendum. Attention has already been called to the initiative and referendum features of the "Commission" plan of city government under the statutes of Iowa and South Dakota. Texas by special act[12] has granted the referendum

[1] No attempt is made to give a complete and comprehensive list; but the strength and widespread character of this movement to secure popular control of elected officials is sufficiently shown by the facts set forth in the text.

[2] Art. XIX., Secs. 1, 2, adopted 1904.

[3] Art. III., Sec. 1, adopted 1898.

[4] Art. VI., Secs. 1, 22, adopted 1900; the state constitutional provision is not self-executing and the legislature has not yet passed an enabling act.

[5] Art. IV., Sec. 1, adopted 1902; Art. XVII., Sec. 1, adopted 1906.

[6] Art. V., Sec. 1, adopted 1906.

[7] Art. V., Secs. 1-8, Art. XXIV., Sec. 3, adopted 1907.

[8] Art. IV., Part 3, Secs. 17-22, adopted 1908.

[9] Art. IV., Sec. 1, adopted 1908.

[10] Art. IV., Sec. 1-a, adopted 1906.

[11] Art. XVIII, Secs. 4a-4e, adopted 1907.

[12] Special Laws of 1907, Chapter 7.

Local Self-Government the Goal 107

to Fort Worth; and Massachusetts the initiative and referendum to Haverhill[1] and Gloucester.[2]

Lincoln and Omaha, in Nebraska, have adopted the initiative and referendum under the authority of a general statute.[3] Montana, in 1907, enacted a similar statute.[4] The right of initiative is incorporated in the laws granting a commission form of government to Dallas, Texas, and Lewiston, Idaho.

Under the home-made charter provisions of the constitutions of Missouri, California, Washington, and Colorado, many cities have incorporated the right of initiative or referendum (very frequently both) in their charters.[5]

Many of the cities in California and Washington, enjoying home-made charters, have also adopted the recall; for example, Los Angeles in 1903, San Diego, San Bernardino, Pasadena, and Fresno in 1905; Santa Monica, Alameda, Long Beach, Vallejo, Riverside, and San Francisco in 1907, Seattle in 1906 and Everett in 1907.

The recall has been provided by statute for cities governed under the commission plan in

[1] Chapter 574, Laws of 1908.
[2] Chapter 611, Laws of 1908.
[3] Laws of 1897, Chapter 32.
[4] Laws of 1907, Chapter 62.
[5] For example, Kansas City in Missouri; San Francisco, Vallejo, Los Angeles, Fresno, San Diego, Sacramento, Riverside, Eureka, Alameda, Santa Cruz, Long Beach, Santa Monica, Pasadena, San Bernardino, in California; Everett, Spokane, Seattle, in Washington; Denver in Colorado.

Iowa and South Dakota, and by special act in Idaho for the city of Lewiston. Texas has granted by special legislation the right of recall to El Paso,[1] Fort Worth,[2] Denison,[3] and Dallas,[4] and Washington[5] in 1907 extended the right of recall in the case of councilmen to all cities of the second class.[6]

Haverhill, Massachusetts, has the right of recall by the terms of the recent statute already noted, granting it a commission form of government. Every city in Oregon may exercise the initiative, the referendum, and the recall.[7]

THE NEW CHARTER PROPOSED FOR BOSTON.

The plan of city government recommended by the commission appointed to frame a new charter for Boston is published as this book is going through the press.[8] The leading features of the commission's plan are: The simplification of the structural plan of the city government; the centralizing of responsibility for the exercise of such powers as are granted the city; the require-

[1] Special laws of 1907, Chapter 5.
[2] Special laws of 1907, Chapter 7.
[3] Special laws of 1907, Chapter 33.
[4] Special laws of 1907, Chapter 71.
[5] Laws of 1907, Chapter 241, Sec. 15.
[6] 10,000 to 20,000 population.
[7] Const. Art. IV., as amended 1906; Art. II., as amended 1908.
[8] Report to the General Court of the Boston Finance Commission, January 29, 1909.

ment that experts shall have charge of the administrative departments; the separation of city elections from all others; a simplified municipal ballot and the abolition of party nominations; the creation of a permanent commission of five residents of the city to be appointed by the governor to investigate the operations of the city government and make reports and recommendations.

Excluding innumerable minor officials and six officials appointed by the governor, Boston's city government when the commission was appointed in July, 1907, was conducted by 242 persons, of whom ninety-seven—viz., a mayor, a two-chambered city legislature (thirteen aldermen, seventy-five members of the common council), a school committee of five members, three street commissioners—were elected at the polls and four were elected by one or both branches of the city council. The remainder were heads of some fifty separate departments. The mayor appointed ninety-nine subject to confirmation by the board of aldermen, nine upon the recommendation of outside bodies, and thirty-three upon his own initiative and without need of other than his own approval. The commission leaves the school committee undisturbed,[1] but reduces the remaining officials to

[1] The school committee of Boston was reorganized in 1905 (Chap. 349, Laws of 1905). It has five members elected by the city at large. As originally constituted, two were elected for three years, two for two years, and one for one year, and

be elected at the polls from ninety-two to ten, viz., the mayor and the city council which is made a single body of nine members, three elected each year by the voters at large for a term of three years.

The mayor has the absolute power of appointing any head of a city department or member of a municipal board subject to these qualifications: "They shall be recognized experts in such work as may devolve upon the incumbents of said offices, or persons specially fitted by education, training, and experience to perform the same, and (except the election commissioners who shall remain subject to the provisions of existing laws) shall be appointed without regard to party-affiliation or to residence at the time of appointment." And the mayor's appointment does not become operative unless at least a majority of the state civil-service commission certifies within thirty days that they have made a careful inquiry into the qualifications of the appointee and that in their opinion he is qualified by education, training, and experience for said office. All appointments are for a four-year term, but the mayor may remove at pleasure.

The annual appropriation bill or budget originates with the mayor. The council may eliminate or reduce but cannot increase or add items. "Every appropriation and every other act, order,

---

it was provided that at every succeeding city election there should be elected for three years so many members as were necessary to fill vacancies caused by expiring terms.

resolution, and vote of the city council shall be presented to the mayor," and if returned within fifteen days " to the city council with his objections thereto the same shall be void." "If the same involves the expenditure of money, the mayor may approve some of the items in whole or in part and disapprove other of the items in whole or in part, and only such items or parts of items as he approves shall be in force and such items or parts of items as he disapproves shall be void."

The mayor and council, except as to a few departments specifically named, are given full authority to organize the entire administrative service of the city and to regulate the salaries.

The mayor at any time may attend and address the city council in person or through the head of a city department or a member of a board upon such subject as he may desire, and the council may request specific information on any municipal matters from the mayor. On a week's written notice the mayor must attend a meeting of the council personally or through a head of a department or a member of a board "and publicly answer all questions that may be asked relating to the subject matter of said request."

Municipal elections are held on the Tuesday after the second Monday in January, and the terms of officers then elected begin on the first Monday of the following February. Primaries for the nomination to elective city offices are forbidden. A candidate must be nominated by a petition signed by 5,000 qualified voters in order to have his name printed upon the official election-day ballot. The names of candidates for the same office are printed upon the official ballot in the order in which they may be drawn by the board of election commissioners in the presence of the candidates or their representatives. No political designation of any sort is permitted on the municipal ballot.

The mayor is always elected for a four-years' term, but at the regular state election in November during his second year of service the question is submitted to the general electorate: "Shall there be an election for mayor at the next municipal election?" If a majority of the voters answer this question in the affirmative, the name of the person then holding the office of mayor (other than an acting mayor) is put on the ballot at the municipal election in the following January. "If prior to October first in the second year of his term the mayor shall file with the secretary of the commonwealth a written notice that he does not desire said question to appear upon the ballot at said state election, it shall be omitted; his term of office shall expire on the first Monday of February following, and there shall be an election for mayor in said city held in January next following said state election." If the mayor then wishes to be renominated, he must file a petition with 5,000 signatures as in the case of other candidates to elective city office.

There is to be a permanent "finance com-

Local Self-Government the Goal

mission" of five paid members, appointed by the governor, one each year for the term of five years. This commission is "to investigate any and all matters relating to appropriations, loans, expenditures, accounts, and methods of administration affecting the city of Boston or the county of Suffolk or any department thereof that may appear to the commission to require investigation, and to report from time to time to the mayor, the city council, the governor, or the general court." If requested by the mayor, city auditor, or the city treasurer the finance commission is also to investigate the facts with regard to any claim against the city and report; "and pending said report payment shall be withheld." The commission is amply equipped with power for all purposes of investigation. It may prescribe reasonable rules for the conduct of hearings; compel the attendance and the testimony under oath of witnesses, the production of books and papers; and procure orders for depositions of witnesses out of the state. The city must appropriate annually a sum sufficient to pay the salaries of the members of the commission and the further sum of at least $25,000; and the commission is authorized to spend in its work "such additional sums as may be appropriated for the purpose by the mayor and city council."

CHAPTER VIII

CITY GOVERNMENT IS GOVERNMENT

THE administrative functions of a city government are so overwhelmingly preponderant that some persons hold that it has no political side whatever. Likening a municipal corporation to a private business corporation and the city's voters to stockholders, they argue that no question of politics is involved in the management of a private corporation and that the consideration of such questions is equally out of place in the conduct of a municipal corporation; that, in short, city government is business, not politics, and that the way of escape from the evils of bad city government is to recognize that all "politics" must be eliminated from its conduct and to treat it as a purely business matter.

All will agree that even a business enterprise must be conducted in accordance with some policy and that some one must determine the policy. If the policy be unwise the enterprise will fail, however honest or capable its administration; and the enterprise will equally fail, be its policy never so wise, if administration of the policy is dishonest or incapable. It is self-evident that no business enterprise is possible without first determining the policy to be followed and then administering the policy determined upon; and that honest and capable administration does not involve opinions by the members of the administrative staff on the merits of the business policy adopted. No successful business man fails to recognize the soundness of these principles and to apply them in the practical conduct of any undertaking for whose success or failure he is responsible. In the business world the distinction between policy and administration is universally recognized, and the opinions of the administrative staff of a business in regard to the policy of the business are not considered to be any part of the proper performance of their administrative duties. The policy is determined by the owners of the business or their duly authorized representatives.

If the business is incorporated, all matters of corporate policy are determined by the stockholders or by the board of directors whom they elect. What the policy of the corporation should be is often the subject of serious disputes. Shall the surplus earnings be distributed as increased dividends or used to enlarge the plant or extend the business? The differences of opinion that such a question will call forth are often very wide and parties will be formed among the stockholders to secure the election of a board of directors that will represent the one or the other policy or some compromise between the two extremes of opinion. Instances of such partisan struggle for control of business policy are constantly occurring. That the question is a purely business one and the corporation a purely business corporation eliminates neither parties nor partisanship.

Nor does any one expect it to be otherwise. It is a matter of common knowledge that any question, the decision of which men believe to be deeply affecting their interests, will arouse partisanship and create parties in the effort to control the decision. If, then, the city's voters are to regard themselves as stockholders of the municipal corporation they will justly feel themselves entitled to a direct voice in the decision of the policy of the corporation and, to choose directors who will represent the prevailing opinion among the stockholders; and parties will be formed and partisanship aroused to give expression and effect to this prevailing opinion.

What is this in essence but politics, and partisan politics at that? Rightly understood, politics is but the application in the decision of questions of *public* policy of the same principles and the use of the same methods that must be applied and used in the determination of the policy of a private business undertaking.

The truth is that city government in its essential nature is government; as much so as a state government or the national government and, like them, its conduct is a public, not a private matter. Like them also, and in this respect it does not differ from private business undertakings, its policy-determining functions are quite separate and distinct in character from its policy-administering functions. Because, however, the chief activities of city government, as of a private business corporation, are on its administrative side, and efficient administration has properly no concern with opinions on those public questions which arouse partisanship and divide men into opposing parties, it must not be forgotten or overlooked that without a policy there could be no administration; that to determine a public policy is politics, and that municipal public policy is not an administrative affair and is not in any sense a private matter.

When we speak of the necessity of applying business principles in the conduct of city government, we are altogether right, if we mean that its policy should be wisely determined and, when determined, should be honestly and efficiently administered by men selected without reference to their opinion of the policy; but we are altogether wrong if we imagine that politics can be eliminated from the determination of the policy, for politics is essential to its determination. Shall a city build a system of docks, establish parks and parkways, construct water-works, own or operate transit lines, undertake the erection of electric lighting and power plants?—these are questions of public policy which will divide the city's voters into opposing parties. These and all like questions are political. The actual building of the docks, laying out of the parks, construction of the water-works, organization of the transit service, erection and equipment of the electrical plants is each a purely administrative matter. Not one of them could be made the basis for any sharp difference of opinion, much less could it arouse any feeling of partisanship. Were the question put to the people, "Shall the docks be built honestly and economically under the supervision of competent engineers?" not a vote would be cast in the negative. Administrative matters involve no question of policy in the political sense, but this in no way diminishes the vital importance of our recognizing that there must first be a policy before there can be an administration of the policy; that the policy-determining function of a city government, as of all government, is a political function and that its exercise necessarily involves the existence and creation of political parties and political partisanship.

There is no difference in kind between the parties created and the partisanship displayed in a campaign for and against the city's ownership and operation of transit lines or an electrical plant and the parties and partisanship in a campaign for and against a protective tariff. The issues, the parties, and the partisanship are political in the one case as in the other. Politics, then, is an

City Government Is Government 119

essential element in the conduct of city government, for the policy which controls its conduct cannot be determined without politics.

The same mistaken reasoning that has drawn from the marked analogy between a municipal and a private business corporation the conclusion that city government is business, not politics, has a striking illustration in the assumption that a private business corporation has no legislative functions and, therefore, that a city government should have no legislative power. This assumption fails to take due account of the principles and methods of corporate management. A corporation acting except in accordance with some corporate policy is inconceivable. When the votes of the stockholders of a business corporation, or of the board of directors whom the stockholders have elected for the purpose, determine the corporate policy, how does this differ in essential character from the determination of the policy of the state by the votes of its citizens, or of the members of the legislature whom the citizens have elected for the purpose? The quality of the act is the same in each case. It is the determination of policy; and this is essentially a legislative function. A czar may determine policy by arbitrary decree, a parliament by enacting a law, the people at large by approving or rejecting a written constitution, and the stockholders or directors of a corporation by adopting resolutions,—czar, parliament, people, stockholders, and directors are alike legislating. Public legislation may be embodied in statutes, private legislation in the records of a corporation,— each is legislation. The argument that because city government is corporate in form it, therefore, needs no legislative power is thus seen to be a pure *non sequitur*, and not the less so even if city government be regarded wholly as a business corporation. For a business corporation must have a corporate policy, or cease to do business; and the determination of policy is a legislative function.

The argument is fatally defective for another reason. A vital distinction between a municipal corporation and a business corporation, as also between the state and a business corporation, is that the former is primarily and essentially public, while the latter is private. The policy of the latter is the private affair of individuals; in the policy of the former, the public is concerned and no one disputes that the determination of public policy is a legislative function. And when democratic principles prevail, just as the voters of a state will, either directly or by representatives responsible to them, determine the policy of the state, so the voters of a city will, either directly or by representatives responsible to them, determine all questions of city policy. Indeed, it might well be argued that, even if the city be regarded as a business corporation, just as its stockholders determine directly by their votes, or by the action of the directors to whom they have delegated the authority, the business policy of the corporation, so the citizens of a city who are the members of the municipal corporation should determine directly by their votes, or by the action of the public officials to whom they have delegated the requisite authority, the policy of the city government (the municipal corporation).

But whether we regard city government as a business corporation or as, what it really is, a public corporation in the conduct of which every citizen of the city has a vital interest, it is certain that in either case it is a corporation; and, since a corporation cannot act except pursuant to some corporate policy, if the policy be not determined by its own members, recourse must be had to an outside authority to determine the policy. This is to put a municipal corporation in a class by itself and to maintain that, unlike any other, it should have no policy of its own, but that one should be imposed upon it by outside authority. The outside authority in this case is of necessity the state legislature.

The choice, therefore, lies between the subjection of the city government to the state legislature —that is, conforming the policy of the municipal corporation to the changing moods of a legislative body which is in no proper sense representative of or responsible to the members of the corporation affected by the legislation enacted—or permitting the city to do its own legislating. For legislation is inevitable in either event.

Each of these methods has been long and thoroughly tried. In the United States, the local policy of the city has been whatever a state legislature has determined. In the cities of Western Europe, the local policy of the city has been determined by a locally elected city legislature. There are few, if, indeed, there are any, students of American municipal history who do not find in the interference by the state legislature with the conduct of local government one of the chief causes of the misgovernment of American cities; and those most familiar with the government of English cities are most certain that a principal reason for its great success, as compared with city government in the United States, is that in England a city is regarded as a self-governing community.

The truth is, city government, although corporate in form, is government; and, while its field of operation is far more limited than that of the state or the nation, just in so far as for any reason it is denied power within that field to exercise its due authority, it is necessarily a failure. The people of a city are as much entitled to determine the public policy of the city as the people of a state to determine the public policy of the state, or the people of the nation to determine the national policy. The wider and wider recognition of this fact is the underlying cause of the growing revolt in so many widely separate parts of the United States against the doctrine, once accepted without question and universally applied, that the city was merely the subordinate agent of the state and as such was entitled to have only such authority as the state legislature might from time to time permit.

As the conception of city government as a real government has gained wider and wider acceptance, there has been a growing realization of the need of making those charged with its conduct more directly accountable to and more surely representative of the people subject to their authority. This explains and justifies the many changes in city charters during the last twenty-five years, and especially in the last ten, looking toward the centering of power and of responsibility for the use of the power. It is to accomplish this purpose, and because it was clearly seen that greatly simplifying the structural plan of city government would be a most important aid towards its accomplishment, that Galveston and the cities which have followed Galveston's lead have centered all power in a small board of directors elected directly by and accountable directly to the voters of the city,—a very strict application to city government of the principles of corporate management. The same simplification of structural plan is strongly recommended by the commissions appointed in 1907 and 1908 to frame a new charter for the government of the city of New York. The commissions agree in urging the enactment of a brief charter setting forth succinctly and clearly the powers granted to the city and in entrusting the exercise of these powers to the mayor and to locally elected bodies, one called the Board of Estimate, to be vested with the city's legislative power as to finance, and the other, called the Common Council, which is to exercise all the city's legislative power not otherwise specially provided for.[1]

Protect the city from interference by the state legislature, clothe the city with ample authority within the municipal field, simplify the structural plan of its government, centre the power and the accountability for its exercise, make it possible with reasonable effort for the citizens of the city to enforce the accountability—were the recommendations of the able men on this commission. The experience of cities the world over has demonstrated that these recommendations are sound.[2]

[1] The Board of Estimate has eight members, three elected from the city at large, and one from each of the five boroughs into which the city is divided; the Council has thirty-nine members, one from each of the fourteen districts in Manhattan, eleven in Brooklyn, six in the Bronx, five in Richmond, and three in Queens.

[2] See report of the Charter Revision Commission of 1907 to the Governor of the State of New York (November 30, 1907); and the Report of the Charter Revision Commission of 1908 to the Legislature of 1909 of the State of New York. The last-mentioned report is not yet (January 29, 1909) completed.

CHAPTER IX

THE RELATION OF THE CITY TO THE STATE

THE city's relation to the state is a dual one. It is a more or less complete local government; it may be one of the state's administrative agents to carry out a general state policy. In each of these relations, because, in theory of law, it is a corporation, the city, during its unfortunate past in the United States, has been the serf of the state, although there is no legal or logical necessity which requires—much less is there any reason of sound public policy which justifies—the serfdom.

The city as local government.

A city like other corporations derives its *existence* and its *power to act* from the state. This is the only fundamentally necessary connection between a city, as local government, and the state. It needs no further assistance from the state. The state's necessary connection with it begins and ends with its creation and the grant of power to act; just as an ordinary corporation, once it is created and granted sufficient power to manage its affairs, has no further need of resort to the state in order to conduct its business. The more completely the central government,—the state,—grants power to the local government,—the city,—to satisfy the local needs, the less occasion there will be for recourse to the state. If the state should grant once for all sufficient power to the city, there would be neither need nor occasion for further activity by the state so far as the city is concerned. The latter, equipped with all the necessary local governmental powers, would perform all the functions of local government. *The city, as a local government, needs from the central government, the state, nothing but adequate power to exercise the functions of local government.*

Nor, if this be done, need there be conflict of authority between the state and city as governments because a city is located within the physical boundaries of the state. The distinction between state and city as governments is not one of topography, but in the subject-matters appropriate to their several jurisdictions, and, when each government has jurisdiction over the same subject-matter, in the extent or scope of the jurisdiction each may exercise.

The government of our federal union and the governments of the states which compose it afford an informing illustration. In the United States, each of the individual states is, of physical necessity, situated within the territorial confines of the nation; yet the supremacy of the national government over the subject-matters properly within its jurisdiction does not at all prevent each state government from possessing and actively exercising absolute authority within its own proper domain. Provided each keeps within its own jurisdictional field there is no sound reason why within the physical area of the city's corporate limits both state and city should not have and exercise full power.

The practical application of this principle does not require much acumen or suggest any serious difficulty. The chief functions of the city as a local government are (1) the determination of the local public policy and (2) the local administration of that policy, *i.e.*, the carrying it into effect within the physical area of the city. Why should there be any clash with the state in the exercise of either of these functions? A state policy is either one that applies throughout the state and is to be enforced everywhere within the state's boundaries or one that is equally applicable to all the cities and is to be enforced alike in each of them; a city's policy is confined within the city's limits and is not enforceable beyond them. A test of the propriety or impropriety of control by the state of the public policy enforced within the corporate limits of a city is this: Is the policy in question a part either of a general public policy embodied in a law equally applicable to every part of the state, without no less than within the limits of the city in question or of a general public policy equally applicable to every city in the state? It is obvious that in the nature of things a purely local policy cannot be the subject of a general law. The mere effort to express a policy suited to the needs and wishes of a particular locality in the terms of a law applicable everywhere within the borders of the state will convince any one of the force of this statement. On the other hand, such a law cannot interfere in any way with a purely local concern. If, then, the state grant the city power to determine its local public policy, no further action by the state will be called for, so far as the city's policy-determining functions are concerned.

But the city, as a local government, has another and most important function to perform. Of what avail is it to the city to decide policy, if some outside authority controls its administration? To every government the policy-administering power is as vitally necessary as the policy-determining power. This is as true of local government as of a state or the national government. For that matter, there cannot be a government without its own administrative equipment to put into effect the policy which it decides should control its conduct. The grant to a city of power to decide its local policy is an empty form of words, unless it be granted also the power to create its own administrative organization to enforce the policy. Until a city have full authority both to decide and to administer its local policy it is not a genuine local government. And just as the easily defined and easily observed distinction between general state policy and purely local policy makes wholly unnecessary any clash between the policy-determining functions of state and city, so, if a city be permitted to administer its own local public policy, there can be no confusion or conflict between the policy-administering functions of the two governments. The jurisdiction of the one government is entirely separate and distinct from the jurisdiction of the other. The city possessed of ample power to perform all local governmental functions can then work out its own destiny unaided and unhindered by the state.

The city can be a truly self-governing community, if the state will permit it.

But is there not conflict of jurisdiction when the state declares a general state policy in regard to sanitation, for example, or the care of the insane or the poor or the preservation of the peace, as to any of which a city may well have a local policy of its own? We know, as a matter of every day experience, that these are among the very subjects with which city government is most intimately concerned; that, within its corporate limits, a city's public policy as to these matters is often based upon a higher standard, and the city's administration of the policy is often more elaborate in its details and more strictly enforced than is requisite in the state at large and may be quite unsuited to the requirements of other cities. As to such matters, it is as much the function of a local government as of the central government to determine its public policy; but this furnishes no sound reason for any conflict of jurisdiction between the two governments.

Let us recall the distinction between a general state policy and a purely city policy. The former either applies throughout the entire state and is to be enforced everywhere within the state's boundaries or is equally applicable to every city within the state; the latter is applicable only within the city concerned. For example, a general state policy as to education, or police, or sanitation applies as well within as without any particular city and will supersede a city's local policy in such matters; just as an act of Congress with reference to a subject within its jurisdiction will supersede a state law on the same subject—*but only in so far as the Congress declares a policy applicable throughout the Union*. Further, the state law is superseded only to the *precise extent* that the Congress has spoken. In all other respects the state law remains in full force and effect. The distinction between the respective jurisdictions is, as has already been pointed out, not merely in the class of subject-matters, but *in the scope and extent* of the jurisdiction. For example, the building of a bridge or the establishment of a market is a city function. The care of the public health is both a city and a state function. The same may be said of the duty to preserve the peace. The state may enforce and administer within the city a general state policy as to sanitation, but is the state not altogether outside of its legitimate field when it goes beyond this point and interferes with the city's sanitary policy of a higher grade, as to which the state, as central government, has no general policy whatever? The determination in the case supposed, (of a sanitary policy of higher degree of efficiency within the municipality,) is as purely an affair of the local government as is the decision of such matters as street paving and grading, the height of buildings, the maintenance of parks, the construction of a bridge, the erection of a city hall, the establishment of markets, the operation of transit lines.

The state government, just to the extent that it has a general policy applicable throughout the state, or to all the cities of the state may enforce that policy within the corporate limits. But beyond this point, or when there is no such general state policy, a city's local policy is not properly subject to state interference or control. If, then, it be asked how, on the one hand, may a city be prevented from encroaching upon the state's domain, and, on the other, the state be kept from intruding into the purely municipal field, or how in any given case shall the line be drawn between the jurisdiction of the state and the jurisdiction of a city, we answer, two things are necessary. The first is to clothe the city once for all with adequate power to exercise all the functions of local government. The second is that, as to those matters over which local government and central government may each properly exercise jurisdiction, the state should not prescribe or attempt to control a city's policy beyond the point required to enforce the general policy of the state.

One wholesome result of the observance of these principles would be to diminish amazingly the bulk of our statute law and to reduce even more markedly the number of proposed laws that constantly cumber the desks of our legislators to an extent hardly credible. During the first weeks of a recent session of the legislature in one of our eastern states more than two hundred bills were introduced affecting the purely local affairs of one city. An even more wholesome and far more important result would be the emancipation of local government from legislative intermeddling with the local public policy of a city.

To repeat, the only necessary connection between a city, as local government, and the state, as central government, is the grant of sufficient power to the city to exercise the functions of local government. The state's necessary connection with the city as a local government begins and ends with the grant of power. When it is recognized that the true relation of state to city is not one of master to serf, it will be much easier to secure both better state and better city government.

The city as an agent of the state government.

The determination of policy by the state government is futile without administrative agents to enforce it; and the state sometimes uses the city as such an agent. The city, therefore, besides being a local government, may also be made within its corporate limits an agent of the state government in the administration of a general state policy.[1] Whether or not the state should use a city for this purpose rather than some other administrative agency will in any given case depend upon its circumstances. It is certain that the power should be exercised with extreme caution and that it often has been and easily can be put to evil use.

The state is under no compulsion to use a city; it may and often does employ other agents for this purpose. For example the state banking, insurance, and excise departments may administer the state laws on those subjects within the municipal limits without resort to any city official.

The right of the state to enforce everywhere within its borders any general state policy is unquestioned. Equally unquestioned is its power

[1] The use of the city as an agent is very common in France and Germany.

to use a city as its agent for the administration of such a state policy within the city's limits. Nor, as we have shown, need there be any conflict of jurisdiction or confusion of authority between the central government and a local government, even though the latter, as the agent of the former, be charged with the administrative duty of enforcing a law which declares a policy as to subjects in regard to which the city may properly have a local public policy of its own,—*provided* the law is made applicable equally and to the same extent everywhere throughout the state or to all the cities alike. The strongest reasons of sound public policy require a strict observance of this rule.[1] That, when the state disregards it, a local government is helpless makes the violation not the less but the greater abuse of power. The evil results of the violation are among the saddest of the experiences of American cities.

There are two other principles of a sound public policy whose observance is of an importance to the public welfare scarcely to be exaggerated. Their constant violation has vastly complicated the city problem in the United States and has been a large contributory factor in the misgovernment of both state and city. The one relates to the supervision and control of a city when acting as a subordinate administrative agent of the central government; the other is the public impolicy of using elected city officials to enforce a state law

[1] This is why the European system succeeds.

which runs counter to a strong local sentiment in the city concerned.

It is elementary that the agent is accountable to the principal for his conduct within the scope of his agency; and, when a city is made a subordinate administrative agent of the state, it is entirely proper that the state should hold it accountable for its conduct as such agent. But the accountability should be enforced by the appropriate administrative department of the state, never by the state legislature. To illustrate, the state department of finance should supervise a city's collection of state taxes, the state health department should control a city's enforcement of the state sanitary policy, the state department of education the city's administration of the state educational standard within its corporate limits.

The state legislature is intended to perform deliberative functions, to control matters of taxation and appropriation; to determine questions of general state policy; to embody that policy in general laws; to create, if need be, state administrative offices or departments. All these are properly legislative functions; but administration, as such, is not a proper legislative function. A legislature is not an administrative body. It is neither equipped nor intended to perform administrative functions. The legislature may properly enact laws establishing the state policy in regard to education, for instance, or the public health, or the custody of criminals; but the administrative service of the state should be left to enforce the laws as to education, public health, and prisons, and the chiefs of state administrative departments, not the legislature, should supervise the state's administrative service. Our legislatures have wrought infinite mischief by intrusion into the purely administrative field. Nine-tenths of the contents of the statute books are made up of details of procedure, of minutiæ of administration. And, since a statutory regulation, no matter how unfit, can only be altered by another statutory regulation, the desks of members of the legislature groan at every session under a stupendous weight of desired and often necessary amendments to the already exaggerated bulk of laws that owe their origin to this form of misdirected legislative activity. That legislative functions are not administrative functions and that legislative activity ought in the public interest to be excluded from the administrative field is a fundamental principle of good government national, state, and municipal.

The observance of this rule is of especial importance in the treatment of city government by the state legislature, for city government more than any other is concerned with matters of administration. Its functions when it acts as the agent of the state for the enforcement of general laws, within the corporate limits, are purely administrative; and it is charged besides with the administration of the multifarious details of its own local business. In the very nature of things its administrative service must often exceed many fold that of the state both in number of persons employed, in the expenditure involved, and in the multitude, the magnitude, and the intricacy of its problems. The evil effects, therefore, of the intrusion of the state legislature into the administrative field are especially felt in the case of cities. These evils are still further aggravated by the fact that the legislature is the policy-determining branch of the state government. The decision of questions of policy gives rise to political parties. Not only is it true, therefore, that whenever the legislature enters the field of administration its intrinsic unfitness for such work results in costly inefficiency—as, for example, when it attempts to regulate the detailed rules of court procedure—but such legislative intermeddling injects partisan politics into the place of all others most unfit for political partisanship—the public administrative service.

This has found abundant illustration in the long history of municipal misgovernment in the United States. Persistent legislative interference with the details of purely local administration has confused and complicated the municipal problem from the beginning.

Whether the general state law which the city is called upon to administer within its corporate limits be one in regard to a matter in which a local government has properly no concern (such as the collection of state taxes), or be one in regard to the public health (for example, as to which the city may have a vital interest in enforcing a far higher sanitary standard than observance of the state law would require), it should always be held clearly in mind that the city has no more lot or share in *determining* the *policy* of the state law in the one case than in the other. It is simply the subordinate administrative *agent* of the state *to enforce the law*, and whether the policy of the same be good or bad, wise or unwise, the state is responsible, not the city.

Now, essential as it is to the successful conduct of any private business that no person shall remain in its employ one instant, if his views as to the policy of the business interfere with the faithful performance of his duties, this is still more essential to the successful conduct of public business. To employ an agent to enforce a policy which he actively opposes is to defeat the very purpose of his employment and in private life is sure proof either of stupidity on the part of the employer, or that he does not want his policy enforced. The same can be said with equal truth and with much more emphasis when the state is the principal and makes a city its agent to enforce a general state law, knowing that, if the elected officials of the city enforce the law, they must pursue a course contrary to the views strongly held by a large proportion of the citizens of the city.

Every principle of sound public policy forbids

any attempt to enforce such a law through locally elected officials. These *local officials* owe their election to the belief that they will represent the views of the local voters. The state, nevertheless, constitutes them *state officials* to enforce a state law that runs counter to the local sentiment. The unwisdom of placing them in such an inconsistent position is manifest from the point of view both of state and city. On the one hand, it introduces the vicious practice of defeating the declared policy of the state by permitting the administration of the policy to be actively hostile to its enforcement; for experience shows that the city's voters hostile to the state policy endeavor to elect local officials who will not enforce it. On the other hand, the enforcement of the purely local public policy, instead of being in the hands of city officials elected on local issues, is committed to persons whose election was due to the local sentiment as to a state policy. We have had many flagrant examples of the pernicious effects of such a course upon both the local policy and the local administration of the city. It demoralizes the conduct of the local government, injects into administration, partisan politics in its worst form and the daily defiance of the law by elected city officials with the approval of their constituents breeds civic degeneracy.

CHAPTER X

THE RELATION OF THE CITY TO ITS CITIZENS

THOUGH the only necessary connection between a city, as local government, and the state, as central government, begins and ends with the grant by the state to the city of the right to exist and the power to act, the connection between a city, as local government, and the dwellers within its borders is of the closest and most intimate sort.

When a considerable population is concentrated within a limited area, not only is there far more frequent occasion for the exercise of all the functions of government within the locality than in a sparsely settled region but the need for such exercise is far more imperative. It has been the invariable experience that the more closely compacted the population, and the more highly developed its industrial organization, the more insistent, the more frequent, and the more extensive are the local demands for governmental activity in the public interest. The determination of the policy which shall control the conduct of the local public affairs, the organization of the administrative equipment to carry out the local public policy, and the establishment of appropriate means to enforce governmental authority within the locality bring into constant use the legislative, executive, administrative, and judicial functions of government. In the very nature of the case some government must exercise these functions. What government, then, shall it be? Shall the city be regarded as a subject province or dependency whose public affairs shall be controlled by the state government, or as a self-governing community, entitled within its local sphere to perform all the governmental functions which the local public interests require?

We are not left to abstract or *a priori* reasoning for answers to these questions. It would seem as if every possible method of city government had been tried in the United States until within recent years, except the one which for three quarters of a century in England has proved itself admirably adapted to the needs of a people whose political beliefs and aspirations are democratic and who during their whole history have been endeavoring through the application of the representative principle to have a government expressive of their will. If we are capable of being convinced by experience, we shall never expect anything but failure from any effort to satisfy the governmental needs of our cities through the method of city subjection to some external authority. The attempt by outside, superimposed authority to direct and control the public affairs of our cities, to determine for them their local public policy and administrative methods, has made an unvarying record of failure.

The municipal experience of Ohio will serve as an example. Ohio is selected not because the attempt to solve the problem of city government by the application of external authority resulted in a worse failure there than in other states—it has been a failure in every state—but because her experience admirably illustrates that, to meet the ever varying circumstances and constantly growing needs of a city, there is no halting-place between superimposed government and self-government. Ohio's experience may also be profitably compared with that of Illinois to which we have already called attention.[1]

In 1870, when the Illinois constitution was adopted, there had begun to be some appreciation of the need of granting to cities at least some power of self-government, as well as of protecting them against the evils of special legislation; and in the Illinois general municipal corporation act of 1872, which was to become effective in any city that adopted it by popular vote, a considerable measure of power to control their own local public affairs was granted to cities. Ohio's constitution was adopted nineteen years earlier, in 1851. At that time it is not probable that many persons actively engaged in political life

[1] Chap. vii., pp. 87-91, *supra*.

The City and its Citizens

in the United States had even begun to think of a city as a self-governing community. A city was merely a subordinate civil division of the state, a part of the state's physical area somewhat more densely populated than other portions. That a city was entitled to be a self-governing community competent to supply its own local governmental needs was an idea scarcely, if at all, present in men's minds. Already, however, in 1851 the evils of special legislation had become apparent and the framers of the Ohio constitution endeavored to check the growing practice of special legislation by requiring all laws of a general nature to have a uniform operation throughout the state,[1] by forbidding any special act conferring corporate power[2] and by providing for the organization of cities by general laws and restricting their power of taxation, assessment, borrowing money, contracting debts and loaning their credit "so as to prevent the abuse of such power."[3]

In 1852 the Ohio legislature enacted a general municipal corporations act which divided cities into two classes, those of the first class with a population of more than 20,000, of the second class with a population of from 5,000 to 20,000. The powers of self-government conferred were much inferior to those in the later Illinois act.

Soon the cities of Ohio began to increase in number and in population and to differ among

[1] Art. I., Sec. 26.   [2] Art. XIII., Sec. 1.
[3] Art. XIII., Sec. 6.

themselves in respect to their governmental needs. The constitution forbade special laws affecting a particular city, yet the needs of a particular city frequently demanded special treatment. What was to be done? The legislature might by amendments to the general municipal corporations act have granted the powers which would enable any city to meet just such emergencies, but this method did not occur to it. On the contrary, extreme ingenuity was used in devising laws general in form but special in purpose. It is altogether probable that in the beginning there seemed no other way to meet the varying conditions and circumstances peculiar to this and that individual city. In the constitutional convention it had apparently been taken for granted that a law affecting all cities of a certain class was a general law within the meaning of the constitution and there was no express limitation to the power to create classes. The legislative method, accordingly, was to create a new class of which at the time there was only one member and to enact a general law as to that class. The court sustained this interpretation of the constitution. And as cities grew in number the classification of cities multiplied.

By the year 1902 there was scarcely a city of any considerable size in Ohio which did not have a charter general in form and theoretically applicable to any other city that came within the prescribed limits of population defining the particular "constitutional class" to which the charter applied. In fact, the city had a special charter which the state legislature had devised for that particular city. There were also innumerable "general laws" which had been passed from time to time to amend and perfect the general law which gave the city its special charter, or which affected in this, that, or the other respect the local affairs of all cities of a particular class, that is to say of one particular city.

The *reductio ad absurdum* of this judicial interpretation of the constitution finally became so glaring that, in 1902, the Supreme Court of Ohio felt compelled to overrule the long line of precedents its previous decisions had established and rendered a series of decisions which left scarcely a city with a valid government when tested by the court's new interpretation of the constitutional provisions adopted fifty years before. So revolutionary was this new attitude of the court that it suspended execution in order to give the other departments of the government "opportunity to take action as to them may seem best in view of the condition which the execution of our judgment will create."

The lesson of Ohio's experience, like that of the contrasting experience in Illinois, is a very plain one. For fifty years the state-government of cities was as thoroughly tried in Ohio as human ingenuity and diligence could accomplish and under the most favorable circumstances. There were very few cities in 1852 when the first municipal corporations act was passed, and Cincinnati was the only city having a population over 20,000. In character they were towns rather than cities; their needs were simple and comparatively few and there was abundant opportunity to learn by experience as time went on. If ever there had been any hope that in practical operation the state-governing method would succeed, or any possible combination of that method with various degrees and kinds of partial local self-government, the utter failure of so highly intelligent and progressive a state as Ohio would have extinguished that hope among observers of comparative progress in city government. How different would have been the story of Cincinnati, for example, if it had possessed even such measure of self-government as was given Chicago by the Illinois corporation act and the courts of Ohio had interpreted the state constitution in 1852 as they did in 1902.

Ohio's experience is not peculiar. The futility of any effort to conduct a city's public affairs without granting to it adequate authority as a local government has been demonstrated again and again. Nor is it any argument against the fundamental soundness of this principle that its full acceptance requires that the city should have a local legislature clothed with complete local legislative power. It is true that city councils and boards of aldermen have so conducted themselves in the past that they have been deprived, with popular approval, of most of such legislative powers as they possessed. But the ill-repute of legislative bodies is not confined to our city councils and boards of aldermen. It extends to the state legislatures as well. How else shall we explain that each new state constitution contains additional safeguards against legislative action? The growing popularity of the initiative, the referendum, and the recall is another symptom of the distrust of the legislative branch of our government.

The disrepute into which the legislative branch of our state and city governments has fallen has not made legislation less indispensable for the conduct of either government. Neither has the reduction of city councils and aldermen to mere simulacra of local legislatures diminished the volume of local legislation.

The local legislative function has been shared in various ways between the state legislature and locally appointed or elected officials and boards, the state legislature itself has been made the chief source and dispenser of legislation for the city, there have been innumerable experiments; not one of them has relieved the city of the need of local legislation, not one of them has successfully supplied that need. A bulky volume could be written illustrating the futility of the attempt to conduct city government without a local legislative body, and showing the confusion and irresponsibility caused by the distribution of local legislative authority among different appointive and elective officials and boards. Contrast in this respect any English city with the city of New York. The sanitary, police, building, street traffic, and other local laws and regulations are within the jurisdiction of the council of an English city. Who will venture to say what or which department or combination of departments of the city of New York has had authority to legislate in such matters? There has been a chaos of local ordinances whose violation may make an unintentional and unwilling misdemeanant of any citizen.

It is time that, instead of curtailing state legislatures of power by constitutional provisions or weakening more and more the local legislatures of our cities, we frankly recognized the true cause of the demoralization and disrepute of the legislative branch of our government and that we began to apply a real remedy.

The popular distrust of our legislatures is due to the fact that their members do not represent the popular will, and, on the contrary, exercise their great powers in many ways that the people positively disapprove. The remedy consists in finding some way to make the legislatures, national, state, and local, representative of the public policies which their constituents desire to have put into effective operation. In the field of local government the application of this remedy depends *first* upon clothing the local legislature with ample power and then leaving the people of the locality to deal with the members of the legislature—witness the experience of Chicago; and, *secondly*, upon adopting electoral methods which will insure that the people of the locality control the selection and election of candidates for the local legislature. Such a legislature will be an assembly truly representative of the local will as to the policies which the city's voters desire to control in the conduct of the city's public affairs. The real trouble is not that there is not abundant need of local legislation, nor that representative government has broken down, but that government, instead of representing the people, is responsible and therefore responsive to interests not in sympathy with the people. Since, therefore, local legislation is a vital necessity, and the transference from city to state legislatures of the duty of providing the local legislation needed has invariably resulted in city misgovernment, we should recognize not only that the courageous and intelligent application of the representative principle in local government is the method which will solve our difficulties, but that there is no alternative.

Every city needs local legislation enacted by a local body clothed with ample legislative authority and locally elected by methods which make its members responsible and responsive to the local electorate.

What has been said with regard to the necessity

of clothing the city with local legislative power applies with equal force to its need of authority to exercise judicial functions. The exercise of judicial functions is as essential an attribute of government as to make or administer laws. A city, therefore, if it be a genuine local government, will have authority to establish courts with civil and criminal jurisdiction as to matters of purely local concern under the laws enacted by the local legislature. If it be necessary to resort to the courts of some other government to enforce the provisions of a purely local law, the command of the law will depend for its sanction not upon the local but an external authority. A community is not self-governing if it has not authority to enforce its laws.

The conception of a city as a mere civil division of the state, to be governed like a subject province by external authority, or, as without more definite status in our political system than the changing moods of a state legislature may give for the time being, must be altogether discarded, not merely because it is unsound in principle, nor simply because it has failed to give good city government, but because it has been the prolific source of every variety of bad city government. In its stead, we must put an altogether different conception, that of the city as a local government; and we must transmute this conception into a vital, living reality. The city must be made a genuine government equipped, as far as the local needs are concerned, with every appropriate governmental power. We must appreciate that, to the extent that a city is not so equipped, it falls short of being a government at all and that the demoralizing intrusion of outside authority into the local field is made compulsory; that there is not a single governmental function whose exercise the adequate satisfaction of the local needs of the city does not make imperative. The city must be recognized as entitled to be a self-governing community, with power to decide all questions of local public policy, power to administer that policy, and power to enforce its authority as a local government; for these are the essential attributes of government. This means that local legislation should be enacted by a legislative body directly accountable to a local electorate and that the questions with which the local legislature is concerned should be limited only by the needs of the community-life which the city calls into being. It means also that those charged with the execution and enforcement of the local policy should be directly accountable to the local electorate. The purely administrative functions of the local government, however, and the performance of its judicial functions, such as the imposition of penalties or other punishments for violation of its local laws, should be recognized as entirely non-political matters. The members of the city's judiciary and its administrative service should be selected and retained in their positions without reference to their views on local or other issues that divide men into opposing political parties.

To sum up: The true relation of a city to its citizens is that of a government, a local government to be sure, but nevertheless a real government; and, as such, it should be clothed with every essential governmental power and amply equipped with the means to perform every appropriate governmental function within its purely local field. But it must be a government responsible to the local electorate. The citizens of the city, the governed, must have full opportunity to enforce accountability for the conduct of their local government. This is democracy, the rule of the people, through the intelligent application of the representative principle.

CHAPTER XI

PRE-REQUISITES TO THE SELF-GOVERNMENT OF CITIES

WE are now in a position to enumerate some of the essential principles to be observed in order to have good city government in the United States.

I

THE CITY AS LOCAL GOVERNMENT

1. *A city is not a province to be administered by some outside authority, but a government.*

Before there can be any successful solution of the city problem it is necessary to regard it from the right point of view. It is self-evident that when a considerable population is massed within a limited area, a community life is developed whose needs and circumstances are very different both in degree and in kind from those of the isolated individual lives of dwellers in agricultural or grazing regions. Who shall supply the new methods and enforce the new regulations which these changed conditions make inevitable? Shall the community supply them or shall some outside authority undertake the task? In other words, shall the central government, the state, control the development of the community life or shall the community meet its own needs? The ultimate authority is in the state, and the community can act in the matter only to the extent to which the state permits. It goes without saying that the state can, if it so chooses, grant to the community no power of self-government whatever. If this be the course pursued, the community is evidently governed as a subject province, the state deciding what is best for it. It is, however, not always so clearly recognized that the community is treated as a subject province when the state apparently grants a governmental power but withholds the right freely to exercise the power, either by not giving the city any means of deciding how the power is to be exercised or by not permitting the city to provide its own means for enforcing the policy it adopts.

Suppose, for example, the state grants to the community the right to build a bridge, but no authority to regulate its use; or to lay out streets, but no authority to regulate the traffic through the streets; or to acquire or establish a lighting plant, but no authority to administer the plant; the state reserving to itself the right of deciding or accompanying the grant of power with the prescription on its own part of the policy according to which bridges shall be built, streets laid out, lighting plants acquired; or, while permitting the city to decide for itself whether it shall have bridges or streets or lighting plants, prescribes the details according to which they shall be administered. Such a grant of power by the state is a mere sham.

The first necessary step toward the solution of the city problem in the United States is to recognize that it is a *governmental* problem, and that, therefore, its solution is not really begun until a city has the authority to *decide for itself* the policy according to which any power granted it, however insignificant or however restricted its field of operation, shall be exercised, and to *organize its* own methods for enforcing the policy.

2. *A city should have all the powers requisite to satisfy the local needs of the community within its corporate limits.*

If the first step toward the solution of the city problem is the recognition that the city is a genuine government, the next is to clothe it with ample governmental authority to satisfy the local needs of the community within its corporate limits. The satisfaction of these needs is the primary function of a city, the fundamental reason for its existence as a local government. If once a city be granted really adequate power to satisfy these local needs, application to the state legislature for the grant of additional local governmental powers will be unnecessary; and if, in accordance with the first principle above enunciated, the city be permitted to determine for itself the local policy and to devise its own methods and adopt its own agencies for the enforcement of its policy,—if, in brief, it be a complete local government, the state legislature will have neither occasion nor excuse for interfering with the substance or detail of the local administration. This eliminates interference by the state legislature with the city problem, so far as a city is concerned with local needs, and makes the city a self-governing community instead of a subject dependency.

3. *Within its corporate limits a city should be invested with all the powers of government not inconsistent with the state constitution or general state laws.*

This simply carries into effect the principles already stated and furnishes a practical method, not only of avoiding any conflict of jurisdiction between the state as central government and a city as local government, but of preserving the superior authority of the state in all matters properly within the latter's jurisdiction. For a *general* state law, if it be defined as one equally applicable either to every portion of the state or to every city in the state, is not intended to satisfy the peculiar needs of a particular locality. Thus a city instead of possessing only enumerated powers would be presumed to have all the powers requisite to perform the functions of government within its appropriate field and something in the state constitution or in a general state law would have to be found in order to overcome this presumption. This would introduce precisely the opposite legal rule of interpretation in the case of a city to the one now in force as to corporations generally—a very wholesome change in the law, if a city is to be a genuine local government.

4. *The qualified voters of a city subject to the state constitution and to general laws applicable to all the cities of the state (and, as a consequence, not liable to alteration or amendment at the caprice of the state legislature) should be free to make and to amend their own form of local government.*

This is a logical corollary of the doctrine of genuine local self-government. No one can become so well qualified by experience as the citizens of a city to know what form of government will be most likely to express satisfactorily the wishes and meet the peculiar needs of the locality. The form of city government best adapted to the exigencies of the local situation must be expected to vary with the special circumstances of each city, and so long as the fundamental principles of the state constitution are observed and the general laws of the state are respected, why should not the citizens of any given city be free to devise the framework of its government? It is generally recognized now as entirely proper that different cities should have different governmental plans, and for half a century our state legislatures of their own motion, or at the suggestion of some one in the locality, have been devising special plans of government for this city and that. New York's charter would be a misfit for Binghamton, the charter of Pittsburg would not suit Wilkesbarre. What sound principle of public policy would be violated, if each of these cities were left free to devise its own structural plan of government? The progressive improvement in the form of city government in the states in which cities to some extent have this power is a practical demonstration of the value of the principle here advocated.

5. *The merit principle should be applied throughout the purely administrative public service of the city.*

There is no division of opinion as to the need of honesty and efficiency in public office. It is impossible to create political parties on such questions as the proper method of building a bridge, collecting the city's taxes, enforcing the building regulations, or a myriad other matters of a purely administrative character. An official whose duties involve in their performance no issue which divides men of different opinions into political parties is a non-partisan, non-political official and should obtain and keep his position because of honesty and efficiency, irrespective of his opinion as to whether the tax rate is too high or too low, the bridge unnecessary, the building regulations imperfect, or as to any other matter of city policy. Experience shows that any other course introduces considerations that deteriorate the city's administrative service in manifold ways. A sure means of making city government extravagant, wasteful, inefficient, and liable to corruption is to permit positions in its purely administrative service to be secured or held for any reason other than honesty, efficiency, and the faithful performance of official duty.

City officials the performance of whose duties involves issues which divide their fellow citizens into political parties are fortunately few. Fortunately, because, if the merit principle be consistently and thoroughly applied to all other offices, the attention of the voters can be concentrated on the few political officers who are chosen to represent the prevailing opinion as to the policy which shall control the conduct of the city's public affairs. This can not fail to make for a responsible and representative city government.

6. *The structural plan of a city government should be simple, centering in a few elected officials responsibility to the people for its conduct.*

One of the greatest obstacles to the betterment of city government in the United States has been the incongruous multitude of elective city offices. It is obvious that the more numerous the offices to be filled by popular vote, the more difficult it is for the voter to exercise any wisely discriminating choice, to have any real knowledge of the relative fitness of the candidates or of the duties and powers of the offices they seek. This of itself is sufficient to condemn the multiplication of elective offices. The evil is further aggravated when the issues upon which a popular election should turn are hopelessly confused by making officials elective the performance of whose duties involves none of the differences of opinion that divide men into opposing political parties. It is an axiom of political science that such officials are non-political and, therefore, should be non-elective. But not only are the voters confused and the issues confused at the time of elections; the evil does not stop with the election. Distribution of authority among a great number of elective offices dissipates responsibility for the exercise of the authority. City dwellers in the United States have become only too familiar with the results of this system, or rather lack of system—a weak and incompetent city government, necessarily wasteful and extravagant, peculiarly liable to become corrupt.

Exactly the opposite course has been followed in England for three quarters of a century and with exactly the opposite results. One of the main factors in producing the relatively better government of the English cities has been that the municipal voter there has been called upon to vote for but one city officer (member of the council) and that all responsibility for the exercise of the governmental powers granted the city has been centered in a single body (the council). This is also the plan that has been followed with success in several of the cities of Texas and of other states which have adopted the "Galveston plan."

It is very easy to determine what city officials should be elected. Only those charged with the duty of representing while in office the declared will of the people, or of taking active part in deciding questions of local political policy arising during their term of office, should be elected. The duties of such officials are political. They should hold office directly from the people and be directly accountable to the people for their official conduct.

Officials charged with purely administrative or judicial duties are in no sense political and should be appointed, not elected.

7. *The successful candidates for elective city office should represent the prevailing local sentiment upon issues of city politics.*

It will aid in accomplishing this result if city elections be separated from all other elections. But, whether so separated or not, they should turn upon local political issues, not upon national or state political issues. The intrusion of these latter into a local campaign should be regarded and resented as an impertinence.

Why do we elect city officials at all? Is it not in order that the government of a city may be accountable to and therefore conducted in accordance with the prevailing local public opinion? And how shall we accomplish this unless we have electoral methods that enable us in city campaigns to give our undivided attention to the discussion of questions of city policy and the selection of men who will after their election be accountable to us for their conduct of the city's public affairs? If these are not the purposes, why should we have any city elections? If we believe in democracy, if we believe that a city should be governed in accordance with the ascertained and deliberately expressed wishes of its own citizens and not in accordance with the views of some outside or superimposed authority, we must be quick to appreciate that the confusion and complexity caused by the multiplicity of elective offices to be filled, and of unrelated political issues thrust upon our attention at city elections, are among the chief obstacles to the city's becoming a really self-governing community, to our having a city government really representative of the prevailing local public opinion.

This is not primarily a question of politics or political partisanship, but a question of doing our duty as voters in a simple, straightforward, business-like fashion. Is it not intrinsically absurd to attempt the selection of fit men to conduct our city government, and to busy ourselves at the same time and in the same campaign trying to reform the nation or the state? Why not admit that it is beyond our capacity to form an intelligent judgment with regard to the fitness of the numerous candidates competing for a long list of offices, national, state and local, some political, others non-political? How can we hope to gain good city government if our minds and those of our fellow-citizens to whom we address our arguments as to questions of city policy are confused by the contemporaneous discussion of questions of national and state policy?

The confusion of ideas caused by the mingling of national, state, and local political issues in the same campaign makes intelligent, not to say discriminating, exercise of the suffrage impossible not merely in the interest of the city, but equally impossible in the interest of the state or the nation. And this is so not because of any criticism of, or any unsoundness in, the political principles of any national political party. It is because it is impossible at the same time to give attention, adequate to the importance of each, to national issues, upon the correct decision of which one thinks the country's future may depend, and to vital questions of city policy such, for example, as the city's relation to its traction companies. The task is beyond human capacity. Similarly it is a matter of ordinary everyday common-sense that the more numerous are the positions for which we are called upon to choose fit candidates the less likely are we to be wise in our selection. This is not because the positions are political, but because there are so many of them. In one of our large western cities, for instance, there was at a recent election one candidate for public office for every five hundred inhabitants. It is the utterly unbusiness-like, wholly impracticable character of such methods that condemns them. The exercise of his suffrage with discriminating intelligence in city elections is an impossibility when the voter is called upon at one and the same time to discuss issues of local, state, and national politics and to examine and decide upon the merits of the long list of competing candidates for mayor, aldermen, city comptroller, and other city offices, besides another list of candidates for county and state offices and perhaps for national office as well. There are too many issues and too many candidates for the intelligent or efficient exercise of the suffrage. It is not at all surprising under such circumstances that men with a well-deserved reputation for great ability and public spirit have openly admitted the impracticability of exercising either intelligent discrimination or public spirit in the selection of the candidates for whom they voted—except, possibly, as to two or three of the long list. They voted as blindly and often as damagingly to the public

Pre-requisites to Self-Government 165

interests as if they were neither endowed with a high order of intelligence nor regardful of their civic duty. Is stronger or more convincing proof needed of the iniquity of such electoral methods than that they have reduced even high-minded and public-spirited citizens to this pitiably helpless condition?

The confinement of city campaigns to the discussion of local issues and to the consideration of the merits of candidates for local office is not hostile to political partisanship, nor does it necessarily involve the propriety or the need of activity by the local branches of national political parties in campaigns for city office. It is simply the application of the practical common-sense business principle that the man who undertakes to do too many kinds of work at once is sure to botch some of them and reasonably sure to botch all of them.

The separation of city from other elections by any appreciable interval will be more conducive to good city government than if combined with the general election held in the autumn; but, when possible, the interval which separates city elections from all others should be at least a year. This has the double advantage of avoiding two elections in the same year and of greatly aiding the exclusion from the local campaign of all political questions and issues that are not local.

Since 1895 city elections in New York have been separated by an interval of a year from national elections, and no candidate for state political office is voted for at a city election except for the assembly—the lower branch of the state legislature. The inclusion of candidates for the assembly among the officials to be voted for has been a very serious hindrance to the complete separation of local from state and national issues, especially in a year when the state legislature will elect a United States senator. That there are also far too many offices[1] to be filled by popular vote is a further hindrance, and the form of ballot required by New York law is actively hostile to the confinement of city elections to city issues. But in spite of these obstacles the cities of New York have in considerable measure escaped from the hopeless plight in which they were under the electoral methods in use prior to 1895. There has been a marked improvement in the character and ability of the higher elective city officials, and in several instances in recent years city campaigns have been conducted almost exclusively upon local issues, with better city government as a result.

II

THE CITY AS A SUBORDINATE ADMINISTRATIVE AGENT OF THE STATE

8. *When a city is made the agent of the state to*

[1] *E. g.*, county offices, such as sheriff, county clerk, district attorney, and members of the state judiciary, as well as strictly city offices.

enforce and administer general laws within the corporate limits it should never be subjected to the vagaries of arbitrary special legislation, but should always be under the supervision of and responsible to the appropriate central state administrative department.

The general laws of the state must be enforced within the corporate limits of the city, and such laws, being general in their nature, must be the work of the state legislature. But the *administration* of these laws is not a legislative function. The state legislature makes the state laws as to banking, but the banking department, not the state legislature, supervises the banks and enforces the banking laws. In similar fashion, the supervision and control of the enforcement of every general state law should be the care of one of the state administrative departments. When the state legislature concerns itself with administrative details, cumbrousness and inefficiency characterize and partisan politics infects the administration.

When the state delegates to the municipal corporation the duty of administering a general law within its corporate limits, the city as an administrative agent of the state is properly subject to state supervision, but it should be administrative supervision, not legislative. The appropriate central state administrative department should be given the requisite authority to compel the satisfactory carrying out by the muncipality of the state policy, *e. g.* the right to withhold state moneys unless the state standard is attained.

9. *If a state policy is repugnant to the prevailing sentiment of the citizens of a city, or of a large proportion of them, the state should not attempt to use the city government to administer the policy; for this means the employment of an agent actively hostile to its enforcement.*

It must be always held in mind that the elected officials of a city, which is made an administrative agent of the state to enforce a state law, are called upon to perform two radically distinct functions: (1) to harmonize their official conduct with the local public opinion; (2) to enforce the state law whether such enforcement is or is not pleasing to the local public opinion. In this latter capacity they are no more city officials than is a judge of the state supreme court, or a sheriff or county clerk. It is not only logically absurd for the state to entrust the enforcement of its policy to agents who have been elected by a public sentiment opposed to the policy, but it is politically vicious and demoralizing.

To sum up: A city should be a local government clothed with ample power to satisfy all the local needs of the community within its corporate limits. It cannot be such a government unless it can decide all questions of purely local policy for itself and organize its own methods for enforcing the policy. The framework of the government of a city should be the one which its citizens find best suited to the peculiarities of their own local conditions and circumstances, but it should be simple, centering authority and responsibility in a few elected officials, and the election of these officials should be separated by a considerable interval, preferably a year, from all other elections to public office. The officials of a city should never be entrusted with the enforcement of a state law whose policy runs counter to strong local sentiment, and whenever a city is made an administrative agent of the state it should be accountable to the appropriate state administrative department and not to the state legislature.

Such a city would have power to solve its own problems. Its only elected city officials would be, for example, a mayor and a city legislature. Its citizens would have only the candidates for those offices to think of at election time, and it would devolve upon these few officials, elected by and representative of the citizens of the city, to devise a local system of administration appropriate to the city's needs. The people of the city would then know with certainty whom to hold responsible for results. They would not have to consult an indefinite number of statute books nor get the help of a corporation lawyer to find out for them— and very likely not find out even then. The mayor would be responsible for the efficient administration of the various departments and could not hide behind anybody; and the local legislature would be responsible with the mayor for the policy pursued in the conduct of the local government. The city would have a simple government and a responsible government. It is not that a city is a business corporation; it is not that its citizens are stockholders in a business corporation; it is that we must apply to our public business the principles of simplicity and responsibility which we apply in our private business.

The local conditions in different parts of the country differ widely among themselves, and the methods to be used and the obstacles to be overcome in the attainment of simple, responsible city government will differ widely in different places; and so, in all probability, will the form of government in which this democratic ideal will be embodied. In a country presenting such a diversity as ours it would be both useless to expect and undesirable to have development according to one model. But the underlying principles of good city government and the need of putting those principles into practical operation are the same in every part of the country and, for that matter, are as clearly illustrated and established by the municipal experience of Europe as of the United States.

CHAPTER XII

HOW THE OPPORTUNITY FOR LOCAL SELF-GOVERNMENT MUST BE WON

IF no outside authority intervened and if the character of a city's government were solely dependent upon the efforts of its own citizens, they would presently find a way to have one admirably adapted to the local needs. A city must win good government through having those charged with the conduct of its local public affairs directly accountable to its own citizens. It must be self-governed, not state-governed. But the city is a corporation and possesses only such rights as the state confers. It is to the state, then, that we must look for the grant to our cities of the requisite power to enable them to be self-governing. The notorious exploitation of cities by the state legislature and its maleficent interference with the conduct of their local affairs have wrought such endless mischief that, at first, it would seem as if our efforts should be directed primarily toward securing amendments to the state constitutions which would effectively prevent this misdirected legislative activity.

Fortunate indeed would be the state and the cities of the state whose constitution guaranteed to each city ample local governmental powers and compelled it to find a way to exercise them without aid or hindrance from any external authority. But it is very rare that any change in a state constitution is needed in order to confer upon a city the right to govern itself or that it would be prevented from establishing its own local administrative system by any constitutional inhibition. There is not a local governmental power which is not already possessed by some city in the United States; there is no sound reason why each city should not have every local governmental power. Every variety of scheme of local government is already in use; no state constitution forbids the adoption of a very simple scheme centering responsibility in a few elected officials. Nor is any constitutional change needed to enable a city to frame its own charter. This can as legally be done by providing for a local charter convention and enacting its recommendations into law as by placing on the statute book the recommendations of a state legislative committee or of a state-appointed charter commission. The separation of city elections from all other elections does not require an amendment to the constitution, unless to make the separation by a whole year's interval.

Just as constitutional safeguards are desirable to protect the fundamental rights of individual citizens, so will they be eminently desirable to protect our cities in the enjoyment of the right of self-government when that right has been won. But the winning of that right, like every political advance in the United States, must be obtained, in the first instance, through an aroused and intelligent public opinion. If a public opinion cannot be developed of sufficient persistence and strength to compel the state legislature to give the city self-government, what ground is there for supposing that a public opinion can be developed of sufficient persistence and strength to induce the legislature to submit for the action of the people constitutional amendments that would give the cities self-government, or that a constitutional convention will be elected whose members will be more responsive to the popular will or more representative of the popular wishes than the members of the state legislature?

The aroused and intelligent public opinion which clearly perceives that it is essential to good city government in the United States that the city should be governed by its citizens, and is strong enough to secure amendments to the state constitution emancipating the city from interference by external authority, will without such amendments procure from the state legislature the enactment of laws that will enable cities to become self-governing communities. And the state legislature that would enact such laws in response to the popular demand for them would submit for the action of the people constitutional amendments to safeguard the cities in the rights thus acquired and to protect them from assault. In its final analysis, therefore, the attainment of good city government will depend upon the extent and sincerity of our faith in representative government and upon how persistently and intelligently we will work to make our government representative, state as well as local. The representative local government which our cities need for the development of a wholesome, self-reliant, and efficient community-life can be secured only as the result of state action in response to a widespread and persistent popular demand. Imperfect as are our present electoral methods for giving effect to the people's will, such a demand will ultimately be heeded by state legislatures and, the right of self-government once gained, such constitutional amendments as may be needed to safeguard it will follow.

Agitation, enlightenment, persuasion, intelligent opportunism—these are the methods through which every political advance has been made in the United States. It is through them that our cities must win the right of self-government. And these democratic methods are effective. Let us take brief note of some of the things that an aroused public opinion has accomplished through legislative action during recent years for the betterment of city government.

Chicago has shown what public opinion could

effect toward democratizing the city government even under an imperfect and cumbrous charter, if the state legislature is permitted neither to help nor hinder. The constitution of Texas in express terms conferred upon the state legislature the dangerous power to make special city charters; Galveston has proved that an aroused public sentiment could compel the legislature to use this power to benefit instead of to exploit the city. Emboldened by the success of Galveston, other cities of Texas have one by one presented to the state legislature an insistent demand for a local government of simple structure and centering responsibility in a very few locally elected officials; and the legislature has granted to each city the *special* charter its local sentiment insisted upon having. The constitutions of Iowa, Kansas, North and South Dakota forbade special charter legislation for cities; but, in response to the popular demand to share in the benefits of what had been accomplished in Texas, the legislatures of those states have enacted a *general law* under the terms of which any city may have a simple framework of government, and the responsiblity for its conduct centered in a very few locally elected officials. Within recent years the people of New York and other states have increasingly resented and greatly restrained the interference by the state legislature with the local affairs of cities, and the chief executives of state after state have been winning popular approval by vetoes of this class of legislation. In Iowa and South Dakota the initiative and referendum are among the charter powers granted to cities organized under the "Board of Directors' or Galveston Plan."

The charter changes adopted and attempted during the last ten years in the wide-spread effort to make city governments more simple in form and more responsible and responsive to the citizens of the city would make a formidably long catalogue. Even more significant has been the steady progress of the movement in all parts of the United States to secure for the city more and more of the governmental powers requisite to satisfy the local needs—the primary purpose for which the city exists as a local government. Speaking generally, it may be said with truth that the more recent the revision of a city's "charter" the more liberal and the more comprehensive has been the grant of power.

These are some of the results that a public opinion which saw clearly and demanded persistently what it wanted, has accomplished in recent years through legislative action without waiting for constitutional amendments. There is no sound reason of public policy why a city should not have all the governmental powers requisite for its healthy, vigorous, and complete self-development. It is certain, as knowledge spreads of the great benefits to both state and city demonstrated by actual experience whenever a city has had these powers, that an intelligent and aroused public opinion will compel our state legislatures to grant more and more governmental powers to cities and to couple with the grant of power the right freely to exercise it.

It is only by democratic methods that good city government can be achieved or maintained in the United States; and the public opinion that obtained local self-government from the state legislature of Iowa by general law, and reduced to a mere formality the constitutional provisions requiring the submission of a home-made charter to the legislature of California for ratification, will incorporate in the state constitution whatever provisions are needed to safeguard the city in the enjoyment of its hard-won rights as a self-governing community.

CHAPTER XIII

IMPORTANCE OF THE ELECTORAL METHODS USED IN FILLING CITY ELECTIVE OFFICES

EMANCIPATING the city from the control of the state legislature and clothing it with ample powers to perform all the functions of local government will not of themselves make the city a really self-governing community. That problem will still remain to be solved.

A city is not a self-governing community if its elected officials represent, in the conduct of its public affairs, special interests or persons rather than the general interest of all the citizens. We must not lose sight of the fact that, when the city has been freed from state legislative meddling and has obtained the right to be a fully equipped local government, its citizens have still before them the task of making that government representative of their will. Until this task shall have been accomplished the city will not be a self-governing community; and this will never be accomplished until some way be found to hold those entrusted with the conduct of a city's public affairs readily and surely accountable, not to special interests or particular individuals or groups, but to the general body of the citizens.

The use of governmental power in the interest of part of the people, instead of in the interest of all of the people, is not peculiar to city government. It is the fundamental political trouble in the United States, the prolific source of innumerable public evils and consequent popular unrest. To prevent the misrepresentation of the public interest through the possession of the powers of government by representatives of special interests is the problem of problems in city, state, and nation. "The shame of the cities" has been more exploited, in the press and by political writers of the day; but there has been as frequent cause for shame, and the shame has been as flagrant, in national and state as in city government. The truth is that authority will always be exercised in accordance with the wishes of those who give and can take away the authority; and the relatively small number of persons who, at any given time, are carrying on the business of government will, of necessity, endeavor to comply with the wishes of those who have put them in power and to whose support they look for a continuance of the power.

Every government, whatever its outward form, is representative. The supremely vital questions are: Of what is it representative and of whom? what are the interests and who are the men whose approval or condemnation determines who shall or shall not wield the powers of government? and through what methods is their determination made effective?—for these are the interests and these are the men who can and do enforce accountability for the conduct of the government.

Confining our attention to city government,— a city is a self-governing community just to the extent that the policy of its government is in conformity with the prevailing local public opinion. And this will be true just to the extent that those conducting the local public affairs may be readily and surely held accountable to the local electorate. In a really self-governing community, this accountability will be complete.

That the city should be granted the right to exercise every needed local governmental power is an essential preliminary. A city government which concentrates responsibility for the performance of all policy-determining functions in a few elected officials, makes all other officials appointive, separates elections to city office from all other elections, and organizes the city's purely administrative service upon the merit system, will be a most important aid. Under such conditions the citizens could always identify the public officers clothed with authority to exercise the policy-determining functions of the government, and therefore responsible for the policy pursued; there would be no confusion of mind or dissipation of effort because of the multitude of offices to be filled at election-time, and the local issues to be decided in the city election would not be likely to be distorted by or subordinated to issues of state or national political import. There could not fail to be aroused an intelligent and general interest among the citizens in the actual operation of such a government; the voters would understand precisely who were responsible for its conduct. But there would still remain the problem of enforcing responsibility to *them* for the policy pursued.

Not even freeing the city from the domination of external authority and giving it a government of simple structure, such as we have described, easily understood by every citizen—that centers responsibility for the exercise of the city's powers in a few elected officials, separates city elections and city issues from all others, and awakens intelligent interest in the conduct of the city's public affairs among the general body of the citizens—will make a city a really self-governing community. There must still be provided full opportunity for the prevailing local public opinion to be authentically ascertained and adequate means to put the representatives of this opinion in possession of the city's elective public offices. No scheme of city government in the United States is worth consideration which does not make adequate provision for the full, free, and deliberate expression of the wishes of the voters and for carrying their wishes into effect. A public opinion that cannot be authoritatively expressed and effectively carried out is, for all practical purposes, non-existent. By whatever route we approach, from whatsoever point of view we study, the problem of city government in the United States, in final analysis, its ultimate solution will depend upon the intelligent application of the representative principle. And to this end the importance of the electoral methods in use for filling city elective offices cannot be exaggerated.

Even under the favoring circumstances we have described, the prevailing local public opinion cannot be authentically ascertained and its representatives cannot be put in control of the city's government, unless the methods by which the few elected officials are chosen make easily possible:

1. That, at any and all times, each nominee for elective office shall be the choice of a greater number of the voters who wish to put into practical operation the policy he claims to represent than any other person competing with him for nomination as its representative; and, afterwards,

2. That, as between the different policies which are urged upon the attention of voters, the policy shall be successful whose representative secures the largest popular support.

How can the prevailing local public opinion as to the policy of a city government be authentically ascertained or effectively carried out unless, first, the choice of representatives of policies competing for popular support and, secondly, the

Importance of Electoral Methods 183

decision between the competing policies is each made by the *voters themselves* after opportunity for full, fair, and free debate? No well-informed person claims that our present nominating and election methods accomplish either of these results, and until electoral methods shall be established which do accomplish them city government will not be conducted by the representatives of the prevailing local public opinion, and the men, in or out of office, who determine the policy of a city government will not be accountable to the local electorate.

The limits of the present volume do not permit setting forth in detail the defects of our present electoral system or the remedies.[1] The purpose now is to call attention to the pressing need of substituting other methods for those which, however they may have suited past conditions, have become the effective agencies through which private and special interests gain control of our city governments. Entirely satisfactory methods may not be easily found, but, in our search for them, we must not hesitate to experiment. We must be willing to put to the test of actual trial any plan which, after painstaking and open-minded

[1] For a discussion of this subject, see *Detroit Conference for Good City Government* (1903), pp. 49–65; *Chicago Conference for Good City Government* (1904), pp. 321–381; *New York Conference for Good City Government* (1905), pp. 97–110, 295–372; *Atlantic City Conference for Good City Government* (1906), pp. 308–387, and C. E. Merriam, *Primary Elections* (University of Chicago Press, 1908).

study, gives us reasonable ground to hope that those who wield the vast powers of a city government will be made accountable to the voters instead of to the representatives—and often the dummies—of private business interests. The evil is radical, we must not be afraid to apply radical remedies. The exploiting of city government for private profit must be stopped; and it will be stopped when a way is found for the city's voters to put in power, to keep in power, and to remove from power the men who run the city government.

Genuine local self-government is the ultimate foundation upon which the entire superstructure of our political institutions must rest in the United States, if we are to retain the measure of freedom we already have and to continue our peaceful progress toward the realization of a government of the people and for the people, through representatives chosen by the people. It is in our cities that the supremely vital problem of making government responsible to the governed must be worked out, and each city that makes a thorough trial of any plan which gives fair promise to aid in the solution is a benefactor to all other cities.

The personal registration laws, ballot laws, and primary laws that have been enacted in constantly increasing number during recent years, and the vigorous movement in widely separated parts of the country for the initiative, the referendum, and the recall, are evidence of the diligent search for some method that will insure that the deliberate will of the people shall control the policy of the government. No doubt still other methods not yet thought of will be devised. Not the least of the public benefits which will result from the grant of complete governmental power to a city within its corporate limits will be the opportunity thereby given to test the merits of plans to accomplish this result, and in the end it must be accomplished, or government by the people will never be attained. If our cities have, as they should, full authority to establish electoral methods for filling elective city office, some method will surely be found, and perhaps more than one, which assures that city government be responsible and responsive to the local electorate. Meantime, and until cities have such full authority, the least that the state can do is frankly to recognize that city elections should turn upon city issues and to make such recognition effective by abolishing, in the case of candidates for city office, the practically complete monopoly of nomination vested by present electoral methods in the local political organizations of national political parties.

Very slight changes in our election laws will go far towards making such recognition effective. In most of our states there is now an official ballot printed and furnished at public expense. The form and size of the ballot, the order and arrangement of the names upon it, the style of the type, the color and quality of the paper, the methods of voting, counting, and canvassing it are all carefully prescribed by law in minute detail.[1] The voter must use this ballot or lose his suffrage. Every candidate for public office must have his name upon it. The guiding and controlling principle of such a law should be justice. Each voter when he casts his ballot is the peer of every other voter; and whatever the political principles of a candidate, or whatever the source of his nomination, the position of his name upon the ballot should not give him an advantage over his competitors.

There are no complexities in the rule to be followed in framing an official ballot law. Simple fair-dealing is entirely sufficient. All candidates for the same office whose names are entitled to appear upon the official ballot should receive equal treatment at the hands of the state. As between candidates for the same office it should be just as easy and just as hard for the voter to perform the physical act of voting for one as for another. The names of candidates for the same office should appear, therefore, upon the official ballot in alphabetical order under the title of the office.

Nine tenths of the complexities and intricacies of our present election laws would automatically disappear if these simple rules were followed. And why should they not be followed, except that

[1] See, Philip L. Allen, " Ballot Laws and their Workings," in *Political Science Quarterly*, xxi., p. 38.

complexity and intricacy of political machinery make for the advantage of the "professional" and therefore of the private interests he represents?

According equal rights, upon the official ballot, to all candidates for the same office would also extend and liberalize the privilege of nomination by petition now usually granted so grudgingly and with many hampering restrictions in order to discourage its use. The very opposite policy should be followed. Freedom of nomination should be encouraged. Nominations to city elective offices are not made difficult because of any sound reason of public policy; nor can any one give such a reason for granting special privileges or preponderant advantages, in the matter of making such nominations, to organizations primarily interested not in city but in national politics. Yet it is notorious that this is precisely what is done by the election laws of many of our states.

Justice and fair-dealing would grant to no person or organization special favors or privileges on an official ballot.

CHAPTER XIV

A CITY'S CHARTER

A CITY'S charter should bear the relation to the government of the city that a state constitution bears to the government of the state. Neither should be cumbered with matters of legislation or administration.

A city's charter should contain a succinct, but clear and comprehensive, statement of the governmental powers granted, with the limitations and restrictions upon their exercise. This part of the charter is necessarily an act of the state and may be either a state statute or a portion of the state constitution. Such portions, if there be any, of the state constitution as affect cities, and such general laws, if any such be enacted as affect all cities alike, should also be regarded as a part of the charter.

A city's charter should also, like a state constitution, mark out the ground plan of the government through whose various organs the granted powers are to be exercised and should provide an orderly and feasible method for its own amendment. This part of the charter is not necessarily the direct act of the state. For example, plenary authority could be granted to the city's voters to frame this part of its charter through methods analogous to those through which the general electorate of a state frame the state constitution. But, whether the direct act of the state or of local origin, this part of the charter should confine itself to designating the appropriate governmental organs, apportioning authority among them, prescribing the qualifications of the persons who are to exercise the authority, and establishing the methods of their selection.

It would be difficult to find anything else which has a legitimate place in a city charter. Details of procedure and the minutiæ of administrative equipment and regulation should be left to the duly constituted local authorities. They are no more appropriate in the organic law of a city than of a state.

That the ordinary city charter is very different neither detracts from the merits nor disproves the soundness of the underlying principles of the charter here outlined. A city, to be sure, is a corporation, but what more is needed in the charter of a corporation than adequate corporate powers and the opportunity for its members fully and freely to exercise them? If this be done, there will be no lack of corporate action to meet every corporate need. And how else shall we awaken enough interest among its members to assure the management of the corporation in their interest? If this be important to the good management of a private corporation, how much more important is it in the case of a public corporation? A member of a private corporation can resign or sell out if he is dissatisfied with its conduct and cannot effect any change for the better, but the city voter has no such recourse. The municipal corporation, if it is to be really self-governing, must be granted adequate power for the purpose and the city voters must be given the opportunity to exercise their suffrage effectively.

A complicated and cumbrous congeries of statutes, falsely called a charter, whose involved and intricate provisions prevent the people of the city from either identifying or effectively holding accountable the persons responsible for its government is an instrument admirably adapted for exploiting the many in the interest of the few. Innumerable amendments apparently in the interest of the many can be made to such a "charter" without seriously weakening the sinister clutch of the few who hold the real power. A simple, easily intelligible charter drawn upon the broad lines here advocated would place the opponents of democracy in the open and without the advantage of concealed weapons. In place of the innumerable and futile controversies about forms and methods, there would be intelligent discussion and effective decision of the important matters of local public policy. Complexity of political methods is hostile to the popular control of government.

Possessing such a charter as is here described, a city will not only be clothed with adequate power to perform all governmental functions appropriate to its sphere of action, but its citizens will have brought home to them their responsibility for the kind of government under which they live and will have opportunity to make it truly representative of their ideas both in character and efficiency.

The course outlined in this and in the preceding chapters, culminating in a charter which, while preserving the due superiority of the state yet sets the city free to regulate and develop its own community life, marks out the road for the solution of both the legal and political difficulties of the problem of city government.

A city thus constituted is not an *imperium in imperio;* it is subject to the central authority of the state in all matters properly within the latter's jurisdiction. But legislative interference is eliminated and home rule is made not only possible but compulsory.

Does any one believe that the citizens of an American city, if free to rely on themselves and unable to secure any help save from their own patriotic efforts, would fail in time to become a self-governing community with an efficient, responsible, well-ordered administration adapted to the local needs?

CHAPTER XV

THE CITY THE BATTLE-GROUND OF DEMOCRACY

THE political forces that resist every advance toward the attainment of government accountable to the people governed and make for the establishment of a government in the interest of a privileged few are nowhere so active or so powerful as in the city. The city itself creates the economic conditions that give these forces full play. The urgent needs of the city's community-life for water, transportation, light, telephonic communication, and similar communal services can only be met through governmental action. The men engaged in supplying these services are necessarily in the most intimate and constant contact with the city government, while the business interests and occupations of the vast majority of men bring them but rarely if at all into conscious relation with the government of the city in which they live.

On the one hand, the satisfaction of urgent community-needs has created a class of special businesses which are made profitable by influencing governmental action; on the other, is the great mass of the citizens to whom any special effort to reach or influence a city official involves business loss. The enjoyers of special privilege have been constantly watchful of the conduct of city government and constantly active in securing the election and appointment of public officials favorable to their business plans. The general body of the citizens, secure under the constitution in their personal and property rights and absorbed in business callings and occupations that neither need special assistance nor invite any interference from the city government, have paid, at most, only so much attention to it as voting for their regular party candidates on election day might require and, perhaps, at times contributing to their party's treasury.

The exploiters of the need for transit, light, and other public services have found in each city a natural ally in every man who desired some selfish personal advantage from its government. The domination of the state legislature over municipal affairs brings to the state capital the franchise seekers from every city, there to work in congenial and unwholesome fellowship with every other special interest in quest of legislative largess. Neither is the hunter of governmental bounty unknown in Washington. His insidious influence has been felt in every department of our government. The same cause, hunger for the enormously valuable special privileges at the disposal of government under modern economic conditions, has been active in nation, state, and city.

The privilege-seeker has pervaded our political life. For his own profit he has wilfully befouled the sources of political power. Politics, which should offer a career inspiring to the noblest thoughts and calling for the most patriotic efforts of which man is capable, he has, so far as he could, transformed into a series of sordid transactions between those who buy and those who sell governmental action. His success has depended upon hiding the methods by which he has gained his ends. All the forms through which the voters are accustomed to exercise their rights have been strictly observed. Untroubled by conscientious scruples, consistently non-partisan, he has welcomed the support of every party and been prompt to reward the aid of any political manager. Step by step he gained control of the party machinery. His fellow citizens have been in profound ignorance that he named all the candidates among whom they made their futile choice on election day.

For a long time our real government had not been the one described in constitution or statute; our electoral methods had long ceased to furnish a genuine opportunity for the expression of the popular will; the actual government had passed into the control of an elaborate feudal system with its lords and overlords, each with his retinue of followers and dependents, all supported at

The Battle-Ground of Democracy

the expense of the public; yet the people were quite unaware that the ancient methods upon which they relied in order to have an effective participation in the conduct of the government and to secure public officials responsible to them and actively concerned to protect the common interest and promote the common good were rapidly becoming mere shams.

In every department of human affairs requiring the exhibition of skill, the expert, sooner or later, inevitably becomes prominent. There was an insistent demand for the expert of every grade from the highest to the lowest in an undertaking involving so much knowledge of human nature, such mastery of detail, so much persistence of effort, and such adroitness as the conduct of government by purchase under the guise of a government by the people. In response to this demand came the "Boss," the expert who attended to the infinite details and complications of party management and organization and supplied the public officials—and thereby the kind of government,—the privilege-seeker desired.

The boss was a distinct advantage to the class that throve by government favors. His real occupation was unknown to the people, and if at first they did not welcome his appearance they thought him nevertheless the natural and perfectly legitimate outcome of their accustomed political methods, a leader whom they could displace when he lost their approval. They did not realize his ominous significance. Gradually it began to dawn upon them that they could neither select nor elect him; that he was not a person, but a system. The individual might disappear or be displaced, but the boss always remained. Not until his sinister figure was appearing in city after city and state after state and even in the United States senate, not until there was overwhelming evidence of a hierarchy of bosses, big and little, did there begin to be a general awakening of the people to the existence of a system wholly mercenary, reared upon the greed for special privilege and the sale of such privilege by the skilful manipulators of the political party-organizations.

The issue has now been fairly made up between Special Privilege and Democracy, between government by purchase and government by the people. The contest will be a long one. It has already taken many forms and will assume countless more. Its crucial battles will be in the city, for there the struggle between privilege and the common good is most constant and most intense. It is in the city that the victory of the one side or the other will be most far reaching in its consequences, for nothing is more certain than that the overwhelming majority of the inhabitants of the United States will be city-dwellers. This is already true of the Eastern states. The triumph of privilege in the city

The Battle-Ground of Democracy

will mean, therefore, that the vast majority of the American people have been made the subjects of government by purchase. And it will mean much more. The increasing domination in state after state of the city "machines" over the state organization of political parties foreshadows the outcome in state and in nation.

If the fight of the people to put down government by purchase masquerading in the forms of democracy can be won in the city and a government accountable to the people set up in its stead, democracy will triumph in state and nation. If the people lose their fight in the city, they will lose it in state and nation. The city is the battle-ground of democracy.

CHAPTER XVI

DEMOCRACY AND EFFICIENCY

MUCH has been said and written about the conflict between efficiency and democracy; and it is a common assertion that the American people care more for efficiency than for democracy.

What is the meaning of efficiency as used in this assertion? Does it refer to the political or administrative side of governmental activity? If to the latter, the experience of history has shown that under governments so different as the constitutional monarchy of England, the German Empire and the republic of the United States the same principles must be applied if the administrative side of government is to be efficient. Whatever may be the methods through which the determination of a government's policy may be made, the principles of efficient administration remain the same. These have already been pointed out. It is absolutely necessary to keep the policy-determining functions of government separate from the administrative functions and to organize the administrative service upon a basis of individual fitness not political opinion. No government, whatever its form or kind, has, or has had, an efficient administrative service without applying these basic principles. It is plain, therefore, that in the performance of administrative functions there can be no conflict between efficiency and democracy as a form of government.

If, then, there is any conflict between democracy and efficiency in government, it must be on the policy-determining side. And there is no doubt about the proper test of the efficiency of a government in this respect. It is to be measured not by administrative success or failure—the quality of the administrative service may be good or bad under any form of government—but by the degree of correspondence of the public policy with the common good of the people affected by it. The fundamental principle of democracy is that governmental policy should be responsive to the wishes of the people, and therefore that the officials who determine the public policy should be directly accountable to the people. If we may trust the teaching of history or our observation of contemporary politics, just to the extent that this fundamental principle of democracy is applied the government is approved by those subject to it, and just to the extent that it is not applied there is popular unrest. The peaceful and successful solution of the governmental problem, at least with the English speaking folk, lies in the thorough application of the sound common-sense business principles upon which success in private business depends to the administrative or business side of government, and in applying to its political or policy-determining side—the method is relatively unimportant, the fact is all-important—the democratic principle that the officials determining public policy should be accountable to the people·

Unless, therefore, they are merely dupes of a catchy verbal antithesis, those who assert that Americans care more for efficiency than democracy must mean that we really think the methods of an aristocratic or monarchical or imperial or some form of government in which the policy-determining power is not responsible to the people are preferable to democracy. Exactly the reverse is true. The American people profoundly believe in popular self-government and are more and more appreciating that the hindrances to its realization are outgrown or cunningly perverted political machinery falsely called democratic. They are trying to substitute other methods in order that they may more surely control governmental action. There is no conflict between democracy and efficiency. There is intense conflict between democracy and the inefficient political machinery it is striving to replace.

The Municipal Program of the National Municipal League

DISCUSSION OF THE MUNICIPAL PROGRAM OF THE NATIONAL MUNICIPAL LEAGUE

AT the joint invitation of the City Club of New York and the Municipal League of Philadelphia, a Conference for Good City Government was held in Philadelphia in January, 1894. Out of this conference grew the National Municipal League, formally organized in New York City in May, 1894. The League, includes in its affiliated membership, the leading municipal reform organizations of the country and, in its associated membership, the leading students of municipal government. At the annual meeting of the League in 1897 held in Louisville, a special committee was appointed "to report on the feasibility of a Municipal Program which will embody the essential principles that must underlie successful municipal government, and which shall also set forth a working plan or system, consistent with American industrial and political conditions, for putting such principles into practical operation; and the Committee, if it finds such Municipal Program to be feasible, is instructed to report the same, with its reasons therefor, to the League, for consideration."

The Committee appointed [1] under this resolution made a preliminary report at the annual meeting of the League held in Indianapolis in 1898, and a final one at the annual meeting of the League held in Columbus in 1899. The Committee did not claim that its report constituted the final word upon the subject referred to it, but its members were convinced, as a result of their studies and investigations, that "A Municipal Program" which would embody the essential principles that must underlie successful municipal government was entirely feasible, and they recommended certain Constitutional Amendments and a general Municipal Corporations Act, as setting forth a working plan or system consistent with American industrial and political conditions, for putting such principles into practical operation. The committee's recommendations were unanimously adopted by the League at its Columbus meeting.

The Municipal Program [2] proposed by the

[1] Its members were Horace E. Deming, New York, Chairman; George W. Guthrie, Pittsburg; Frank J. Goodnow, New York; Charles Richardson, Philadelphia; Leo S. Rowe, Philadelphia; Albert Shaw, New York; and Clinton Rogers Woodruff, Philadelphia.

[2] The volumes containing the reports of the Indianapolis and Columbus meetings of the National Municipal League and a special volume issued by the League in 1900 under the title "A Municipal Program" and containing the full text of the committee's report are now out of print. For that reason and by arrangement with the League there is now published at the end of this volume a second edition of the Constitutional Amendments and the General Municipal

National Municipal League may be conveniently considered under the following general divisions:

1. Powers granted to the municipal corporation;
2. The relation of city government to the state government;
3. The structural plan of the city government and in connection therewith the provisions intended to restrict and, as far as possible, to prevent the performance of the non-political administrative functions of city government by those charged with the exercise of its political functions;
4. The methods of filling elective city offices;
5. Various special provisions.

1. *Powers of the municipal corporation.*

Every city within the state is vested with power to acquire, hold, manage, control, and dispose of property. Within its corporate limits, it has the same powers of taxation as are possessed by the state; it may license and regulate all trades, occupations, and businesses, and is vested with power to perform and render all public services, and with all powers of government, subject to such limitations as may be contained in the constitution and laws of the state, applicable either to all the inhabitants of the state or to all the cities of the state, or in special laws applicable to less

---

Corporations Act which together constitute the "Municipal Program."

than all cities of the state if they are enacted in accordance with the following requirements:

Special laws must receive the affirmative vote of two thirds of all the members of the Legislature, and are not valid in any city unless they receive the formal approval of its Council within sixty days after their passage by the Legislature, or, within thirty days after disapproval by the Council of the city, are again passed by the Legislature by the affirmative vote of two thirds of all the members of the Legislature, which two thirds must include three fourths of the members of the Legislature from districts outside of the city or cities to be affected. The failure of the Council of the city to take formal action approving or disapproving a special law is deemed a disapproval. Laws repealing such special laws may be passed in the manner provided for the passage of general laws.[1]

Cities are authorized to establish minor courts, having exclusive civil and criminal jurisdiction in the first instance for the enforcement of city ordinances and of penalties for their violation and such further or other jurisdiction as may be conferred by the Legislature, subject to the other provisions of the constitution, but they can not have any equity jurisdiction, nor any greater jurisdiction in other respects than is conferred

[1] Article Third, Sec. 7 of Constitutional Amendments. Article II., Secs. 1, 2, 3, 4, 5, 6, 7, 8, 12 of Municipal Corporations Act.

upon some lower court recognized as a regularly constituted part of the state's judicial system. No one is eligible to appointment as justice of the city court unless he has been for at least five years a member of the bar in good standing. Such justices are subject to the same liabilities, and their judgments and proceedings are reviewed in the same manner and to the same extent as is now or may be provided by law in the case of the lower state court specified. The justices of such courts and, except as otherwise provided in the constitution, all other city judicial officers are appointed by the Mayor, and may be removed by him in the same manner as officers in the subordinate administrative service of the city.[1]

The intent of these provisions is to accomplish two main purposes: first, to clothe the city government with such broad powers as will enable it to perform all the appropriate functions of a local government without resort to the state legislature for the grant of additional power; and, secondly, to prevent the interference by the state legislature with the free exercise by the city of the governmental powers granted it. The mere grant of the powers needed accomplishes the first of these purposes; the second is sought to be accomplished by defining special legislation and providing that such legislation in order to be valid must first

[1] Article Third, Section 5 of Constitutional Amendments. Article II., Section 9 of Act.

secure the favorable vote of two thirds of all the members of the state legislature and then, unless also approved by the city legislature, secure a second time the affirmative vote of two thirds of all the members of the state legislature, which two thirds must include three fourths of the members from districts outside of the city or cities affected. The state legislature, however, is left entirely free to enact general laws, *i. e.*, laws applicable either to all the inhabitants of the state or to all the cities of the state. Under these constitutional definitions the peculiar needs of an individual city will be met by its own local legislative body, while the laws embodying a general state policy affecting all cities will be enacted by the state legislature; and, if there should be a case which requires special legislation for a city, such legislation will be had either upon the application or with the approval of the city authorities.

The Legislature is directed to pass a general Municipal Corporations Act applicable to all the cities in the state which shall, by popular vote, determine to adopt it.[1]

2. *The relation of the city government to the state government.*

The portions of the "Municipal Program" we have summarized establish the city as a local government and safeguard it in the exercise

[1] Article Third, Sec. 8, Const. Amdt.

Discussion of Municipal Program

of every appropriate local governmental function while preserving to the state its due superiority in all matters of general state policy. The Program also specifically provides in the Corporations Act that within its corporate limits every city shall be the local agent of the state government for the enforcement of state laws except when otherwise specifically provided by a general law applicable to all cities of the state (Art. II., § 16); and, further, that the city shall, in the exercise of the powers conferred by the Act, be subject to the supervision and control of state administrative boards and officers authorized for the purpose by general laws applicable to all cities within the state (Art. II., § 17).

3. *The structural plan of the city government; and in connection therewith, the provisions intended to restrict and, as far as possible, to prevent the performance of the non-political administrative functions of city government by those entrusted with the exercise of its political functions.*

The proposed constitutional amendments[1] require that, in the organization of every city, provision shall be made for a Council, whose members shall be elected by the people, and for a Mayor also elected by the people. These are the only city officers elected by popular vote.

[1] Article Third, Sec. 6, Const. Amdt.

The Council and Mayor. The Council, except as otherwise provided, exercises all powers conferred upon the city subject to the veto of the Mayor, and if there be a sufficient majority may override his veto.[1] The Council has ample power to investigate any department of the city government and the official acts and conduct of any city officer.[2] All sessions of the Council and of its committees are public.[3] The Council may establish any department or office that it deems necessary or expedient for the conduct of the city's business or government. The Mayor, however, fills by appointment all offices established by the Council except that the Council elects its own officers.[4]

The Council consists of at least nine and not more than fifty members, the precise number being determined by the local conditions of each state. Members of the Council are elected at large for six years, one third going out of office every two years.[5] The Mayor is the chief executive officer of the city, and appoints and removes all heads of departments in the administrative service of the city, except the head of the Finance Department, who shall be known as the Controller. All persons in the administrative service of the city, except the Mayor, hold their offices without

[1] Article V. Sec. 1; Art. III., Sec. 6, Act.
[2] Article V., Sec. 9; Art. III., Sec. 6, Act.
[3] Article V. Sec. 7, *id.*   [4] Article V., Sec. 8, *id.*
[5] Article V., Sec. 2, *id.*

fixed terms. The Mayor is given ample power to investigate in person or by agent into the affairs of any department of the city government and the official acts and conduct of any official in the administrative service of the city. For the purpose of such investigation the Mayor, or his agent, can compel the attendance and testimony of witnesses and the production of books and papers. Wilful false swearing in such investigation is punishable as perjury.[1]

The Mayor must from time to time make such recommendations to the Council as he may deem to be for the welfare of the city, and he must submit the annual budget of current expenses to the Council, which may reduce or strike out (but may not increase) any item.[2]

The term of the Mayor is made two years.[3] He may be removed by the Governor after being given opportunity to be heard. The proceedings upon such removal are public, and a full detailed statement of the reasons for such removal are filed by the Governor in the office of the Secretary of State, and are made a matter of public record. The decision of the Governor when filed with the reasons therefor is final. The Governor may, pending the investigation, suspend the Mayor for a period of thirty days.[4]

The City Controller.—Under the plan proposed

[1] Article IV., Sec. 17, Corp. Act.
[2] Article III., Sec. 7, *id.*   [3] Article III., Sec. 1, *id.*
[4] Article III., Sec. 4, *id.*

by the National Municipal League, the general control and supervision of all the fiscal affairs of the city will be exercised by a city Controller. The Controller audits all claims against the city, is responsible for the methods and the correctness of the city's bookkeeping, for the completeness and accuracy of the statements of the city's financial condition, and must make full and detailed reports of the city's financial transactions. He supervises the disbursement of city funds and the accounts of grantees of franchises from the city.

The Controller's is in no sense a partisan political office. His duties are purely administrative and, therefore, he should not be elected by popular vote.

It is to him that the citizens look to prevent the misapplication of city revenues by any of the city's officers, including the Mayor and the Mayor's appointees. He should, therefore, not be himself appointed by the Mayor.

The Act therefore provides for his election by the Council, which may also by resolution remove him.[1] But his term of office is indefinite and the successful performance of his duties requires so high an order of skill and technical training that the impartial and efficient conduct of his office should assure that such a resolution would be of rare occurrence. The temporary tenures and the shifting personalities of their fiscal officers have

[1] Article VI., *id.*

been a most demoralizing factor in the financial affairs of cities.

The subordinate administrative service.—Appointments and promotions in the subordinate administrative service of the city, including laborers, must be made solely according to fitness, which must be ascertained, so far as practicable, by examinations that, so far as practicable, must be open competitive examinations.[1] This is the "Merit Principle," and the Act establishes the administrative machinery approved by long experience for putting it into effective operation.[2]

No one in the administrative service of the city can be removed, reduced in grade or salary, or transferred because of his religious or political beliefs or opinions, or without first having received a written statement setting forth the reasons for the removal, reduction, or transfer. If he so desires, such statement, together with his reply thereto, is made a matter of public record. Subject to this limitation, all persons in the administrative service hold their offices without fixed terms and subject to the pleasure of the Mayor.[3]

The government of English cities is successfully conducted by a central board of directors called the Council. The Mayor is merely presiding officer of the board. The Council has both legislative and administrative powers, but as a matter of fact the Council of an English city does not

[1] Article Third, Sec. 6, Const. Amdt.
[2] Article IV., Act.   [3] Article IV., Sec. 16, *id.*

concern itself with the details of administration. These are cared for by a permanent non-partisan administrative force in which intelligence, technical training, and experience, may find an assured career. Legislative bodies in the United States have pursued an entirely different course. They have devoted a large part of their energies to the details of administrative work. The consequent injection of political partisanship into administration has been and still is a constant and prolific source of many public evils. The National Municipal League, therefore, in selecting a structural plan or scheme of government for American cities, deemed it wise to provide by positive enactment against undue legislative activity in purely administrative work and to make the Mayor the administrative head of the city government. According to the Municipal Program the Council controls the public expenditures and has searching powers of investigation into the conduct of every public office. The responsibility for an adequate administrative equipment adapted to the needs of the city government rests with the Council, which may establish any city department or office it deems necessary or proper. Except the Mayor and members of the Council, every city officer is appointed and holds his office for an indefinite term. The Council appoints and removes its own officers and the city Controller; all other officers are appointed and removed by the Mayor (except that laborers may be appointed and removed by the

Discussion of Municipal Program 215

heads of departments in which they serve). The responsibility for the performance of the executive and administrative functions of the city government is thus centered in the Mayor. Without, however, in any way relieving him from this responsibility, there are a number of checks to the arbitrary use of his power. Appointments in the subordinate administrative service must be made in accordance with rules and regulations based upon the merit principle, and the Mayor is required to establish a board of municipal civil service commissioners to prescribe, amend, and enforce such rules and regulations. The political and religious beliefs of a city officer can not be made the ground for his removal, but there are no other restrictions provided a written statement is made setting forth in detail the reasons, which, at the option of the removed official, must, together with his reply, become a public document. The heads of city departments are removable at the absolute pleasure of the Mayor; but there is no sound motive for their removal so long as they are efficient public servants; and, as is shown by the experience of New York City, the fact that their terms of office are indefinite will tend more and more to the retention of men who are performing the duties of their positions to the general satisfaction of the public.[1] Making all non-

[1] The New York City charter, which went into effect January 1, 1901, provided that the heads of the city's great administrative departments should be appointed without fixed terms.

political offices appointive, with tenure during good behavior and so long as official duties are performed with diligence and competence, will attract to the public service the intelligence, the technical skill, and the experience of which there is more and more pressing need in the administrative work of our cities.

Every two years the citizens elect the Mayor and one third of the Council. The holding of city elections at intervals of two years makes possible their separation from national and state elections. The voters at city elections can give their undivided attention to local political issues. The Mayor's veto power in local legislation and his importance as the head of the administrative service, will make certain that at each election there will be a thorough discussion and review of the manner in which the city government is conducted. Since there are only two officers to be elected,—the Mayor and members of the Council,—and these have the entire responsibility for the manage-

---

This was the first statutory recognition in the United States of the wisdom of the practice that has been one of the important contributory causes of the superior efficiency of the administrative service of the European cities. The chief of an administrative department in a European city is appointed because he is an expert in the line of work his department is expected to do, and holds his position indefinitely. The political opinions of the majority of the Council of an English city, for example, have no influence whatever upon the tenure of the officer in charge of its water department. This is solely dependent upon the continued display of his competence as an expert administrator.

Discussion of Municipal Program

ment of the city government, the voters will not be confused by the multitude of offices to be filled.

4. *The methods of filling elective city offices.*

The proposed Constitutional Amendments[1] require the enactment of laws providing for the ascertainment by proper proof of the citizens entitled to vote, for the personal registration of voters and for absolute secrecy in voting. The election of city officers is required to be at a different date from that of any election of officers of the state or national government.

With candidates for only two offices to be voted for, Mayor and members of the Council, the election methods can be made very simple. Nominations of elective city officers are by petition signed by qualified voters of the city. The Council may determine the number of signatures, but not more than fifty signatures shall be required. The petition must be filed in the Mayor's office at least thirty days prior to the date of the election, except in the case of the death or withdrawal of a candidate. The voter must vote separately for each candidate for whom he desires to vote. If the election is by ballot, the Council may determine the form of the ballot, but the names of all candidates for the same city office must be printed upon the ballot in alphabetical order under the title of the office.[2] The nominating petitions need

[1] Article First, Const. Amdt.
[2] Article First, Const. Amdt., Sec. 3; Art. VII., Sec. 2, Act.

not be one paper and may be written or printed, but the signatures thereto must be the genuine autographs of the persons whose names purport to be signed. The house address of the signer must be added and the signature must be made and acknowledged or proved before an officer authorized to take acknowledgments and proof of deeds. The certificate of the officer is sufficient proof of the genuineness of the signature for the purpose of the petition, but signing another's name or a false or fictitious name, or signing a certificate falsely stating that a signature was made in the presence of the officer or acknowledged or proved before him, is made a felony.[1]

ADDITIONAL FEATURES.

There are a number of other important features of the Municipal Program to which attention should be called.

Initiative, Referendum, Recall, Proportional Representation.

Under Article Third, Section 7, of the proposed Constitutional Amendments, a city may adopt the initiative, the referendum, and the recall.[2] The power to establish direct legislation and minority or proportional or other method of representation is specifically conferred by Section 3 of

---

[1] Article Fifth., Const. Amdt.; Art. VII., Sec. 4, Act.
[2] See also Article Fourth, Const. Amdt.

the same article. These may be established in any city by the Council with the consent of the majority of the qualified voters of the city. On a petition therefor signed by two per cent. of the qualified voters of the city (there must be not less than one thousand signers), the Council must submit to popular vote at the next ensuing election a proposition to establish the initiative, the referendum, minority or proportional or other method of representation.

Actions by citizens.

Under the provisions of the Municipal Program any citizen who is a householder of the city—upon giving, if required by the court, security to indemnify the city against costs—may maintain an action in the name of the city to restrain the execution of any illegal, unauthorized, or fraudulent contract on behalf of the city; or the payment of any illegal, unauthorized, or fraudulent claims against the city; or to compel the refunding of any illegal, unauthorized, or fraudulent payment on behalf of the city (Art. VII., Sec. 1, Act).

Franchises.

The Municipal Program has laid down certain fundamental principles to be observed in dealing with grants to individuals or corporations to perform such public services as the furnishing of light, power, water, transit, to the city or its inhabitants.

The city is given power to decide for itself, as fully and as freely as the state now decides, all questions in regard to the performance of such public services.[1] Whether and to what extent the city should itself render such services, or any of them, or should grant the right to others, is left for local determination. The city is thus placed in a position where it is not obliged to go without electric light, for instance, unless it will submit to such terms as a private corporation may see fit to impose in the absence of any real competition. This is the first fundamental principle. The city is made free to decide its policy without resort to any outside authority.

In the second place,[2] the rights of every city in and to its water front, ferries, wharf property, land under water, public landings, wharves, docks, streets, avenues, parks, bridges, and all other public places, are declared to be inalienable, except by a four-fifths vote of all the members elected to the Council approved by the Mayor; and no franchise, lease, or right to use the same, either on, through, across, under, or over them, and no other franchise granted by a city, to any private corporation, association, or individual, shall be for a longer period than twenty-one years.

In the third place,[2] such grant and any contract in pursuance thereof may provide that upon the

[1] Art. Third, Sec. 7, Const. Amdt.; Art. II, Secs. 1 and 10, Act.

[2] Art. Third, Sec. 1, Const. Amdt.; Art. II., Sec. 10, Act.

termination of the grant, the plant, as well as the property, if any, of the grantee in the streets, avenues, and other public places shall thereupon without further or other compensation to the grantee, or upon the payment of a fair valuation thereof, be and become the property of the city; but the grantee shall be entitled to no payment because of any valuation derived from the franchise. Every grant shall specify the mode of determining any valuation therein provided for, and shall make adequate provision by way of forfeiture of the grant, or otherwise, to secure efficiency of public service at reasonable rates, and for the maintenance of the property in good order throughout the term of the grant.

In the fourth place,[1] every grantee of such franchises or rights to use shall keep books of accounts and make stated quarterly reports in writing to the city Controller. The books must be kept and the reports made in accordance with forms and methods prescribed by him, which, so far as practicable, shall be uniform for all such grantees. The Controller may inspect and examine, or cause to be inspected or examined, at all reasonable hours, the books of account of the grantee. The reports must contain an accurate statement, in summarized form and also in detail, of all financial receipts from all sources, and all expenditures for all

[1] Art. Third, Sec. 1, Const. Amdt.; Art. II., Sec. 10, Act.

purposes, together with a full statement of assets and debts and such other information as to the financial condition of the grantee as the Controller may require. These reports are public documents.[1] The Controller is required to keep a separate record for each grantee showing:

1. The true and entire cost of construction, of equipment, of maintenance, and of the administration and operation thereof; the amount of stock issued, if any; the amount of cash paid in, the number and par value of shares, the amount and character of indebtedness, if any, the rate of taxes, the dividends declared, the character and amount of all fixed charges, the allowance, if any, for interest, for wear and tear or depreciation, all amounts and sources of income;

2. The amount collected annually from the city treasury and the character and extent of the service rendered therefor to the city;

3. The amount collected annually from other users of the service and the character and extent of the service rendered therefor to them. Such books of record shall be open to public examination at any time during the business hours of the Controller's office.[2]

The city's power to incur indebtedness.

It is usual in the United States to limit the power of a city to incur indebtedness to a given

[1] Art. II., Sec. 10, Act. [2] Art. VI., *id*.

Discussion of Municipal Program

percentage of the assessed valuation of taxable real estate within the corporate limits. The Municipal Program retains this principle as to all debts incurred by the city for any purpose or undertaking which is not completely self-supporting. But it makes a distinction between such debts and a debt incurred to supply the city with water, for example, or for any other specific undertaking from which is derived a revenue sufficient to make the enterprise completely self-sustaining and to amortize the principal of the debt at or before its maturity. The framers of the Municipal Program recommend that bonds issued to establish completely self-sustaining enterprises should not be included within the city's debt limit.

New York City's experience has furnished convincing proof of the soundness of the recommendation. The income from the users of the city water has been more than enough to pay the interest charges, amortize the principal of the debt, and meet the expenses of maintenance and operation, besides making ample provision for replacement of the plant. The resources of the city have not been diminished, they have been increased by the ownership and operation of the water-works. Yet in the determination of the city's debt limit the water bonds were until recently placed upon precisely the same footing with bonds necessarily paid, principal and interest, from the proceeds of taxation. The city has been in the same situation as to the bonds issued to build subways for rapid transit. In this instance the city retained the ownership of the roads and contracted for the construction and operation. The performance of the contract is amply secured. At the termination of the contract the bonds will have been paid in full and meantime not a penny of expense for interest or for the maintenance or operation of the subway will have come from the pockets of the city taxpayer. The Financial Department has long represented that the entire expense of improving the city's docks is more than met by the revenues received from their users. These instances are sufficient to show that city bonds issued for improvements necessarily paid from the proceeds of taxation and those issued for improvements which cost the taxpayer nothing do not properly belong in the same category. Under proper safeguards, bonds of the latter class should be excluded in determining the limitation of a city's power to incur indebtedness.

The provisions of the Municipal Program[1] in this respect are the following:

The bonds issued for such an undertaking must be authorized by the affirmative vote of two thirds of the Council and approved by the Mayor and by the affirmative vote of the majority of the qualified voters of the city voting upon the question of their issuance at the next ensuing election. From and after a period to be determined by the Council,

[1] Art. Third, Sec. 2 (2), Const. Amdt.

not exceeding five years from the date of such election, whenever and for so long as such an undertaking fails to produce sufficient revenue to pay all costs of operation and administration (including interest on the city's bonds issued therefor and the cost of insurance against losses by fire, accidents, and injuries to persons) and an annual amount sufficient to pay at or before maturity all bonds issued on account of said undertaking, all such bonds outstanding shall be included in determining the limitation of the city's power to incur indebtedness, unless the principal and interest thereof be payable exclusively from the receipts of such undertaking. The City Controller shall annually report to the Council in detail the amount of the revenue from each such undertaking and whether there is any and, if so, what deficit in meeting the requirements above set forth.

Provision shall be made at the time of their issue for raising a sum of money by taxation sufficient to pay, as it falls due, the interest upon all city bonds not exclusively payable from the receipts of revenue-producing undertakings, and to pay and discharge the principal thereof within —— years from the date of their issue; but whenever in any year the receipts from any revenue-producing undertaking shall be sufficient to pay the costs of operation and administration as above defined, and the annual amount hereinbefore required, the tax to pay the interest and provide for the principal of the bonds issued for such undertaking shall not be collected, and the same shall be paid from such receipts.[1]

[1] Recent amendments to the New York constitution exempt from the constitutional debt limit New York City water bonds

Municipal Accounts.

The Municipal Program does not attempt to prescribe in detail just what the city's books of account should contain nor how they should be

---

issued after January 1, 1904, and the water bonds of cities of the second class issued after January 1, 1908. A similar amendment is pending relating to water bonds of cities of the third class. The New York legislature at its session in 1908 passed the following proposed amendment to the state constitution: ". . . any debt hereafter incurred by the City of New York for a public improvement owned or to be owned by the city, which yields to the city current net revenue after making any necessary allowance for repairs and maintenance for which the city is liable, in excess of the interest on said debt and of the annual instalments necessary for its amortization, may be excluded in ascertaining the power of said city to become otherwise indebted, provided that a sinking fund for its amortization shall have been established and maintained and that the indebtedness shall not be so excluded during any period of time when the revenue aforesaid shall not be sufficient to equal the said interest and amortization instalments, . . . any indebtedness heretofore incurred by the City of New York for any rapid transit or dock investment may be so excluded proportionately to the extent to which the current net revenue received by said city therefrom shall meet the interest and amortization instalments thereof, provided that any increase in the debt incurring power of the City of New York which shall result from the exclusion of debts heretofore incurred shall be available only for the acquisition or construction of properties to be used for rapid transit or dock purposes. The legislature shall prescribe the method by which and the terms and conditions under which the amount of any debt to be so excluded shall be determined, and no such debt shall be excluded except in accordance with the determination so prescribed. The legislature may in its discretion confer appropriate jurisdiction on the appellate division of the supreme court in the first judicial department for the purpose of determining the amount of any debt kept, but it sets forth the fundamental principles which, if intelligently applied, would enable the financial condition of the city's government and the quality of the administration of the city's public business to be as thoroughly known and as accurately tested as are the financial condition and business administration of any well managed large private corporation.

All the cities of the state are required by Article Third, Sec. 4, of the proposed constitutional amendments to make stated annual reports to the state fiscal officer in accordance with forms and methods prescribed by him, which must be uniform for all cities. These reports are printed as public documents and must disclose fully, and in both summarized form and in detail:

1. The receipts from all sources and expenditures for all purposes;

---

to be so excluded. No indebtedness of a city valid at the time of its inception shall thereafter become invalid by reason of the operation of any of the provisions of this section."

Article VIII., Section 24, of the Michigan constitution adopted in 1908 reads: "When a city or village is authorized to acquire or operate any public utility, it may issue mortgage bonds therefor beyond the general limit of bonded indebtedness prescribed by law: Provided, That such mortgage bonds issued beyond the general limit of bonded indebtedness prescribed by law shall not impose any liability upon such city or village, but shall be secured only upon the property and revenues of such public utility, including a franchise stating the terms upon which, in case of foreclosure, the purchaser may operate the same, which franchise shall in no case extend for a longer period than twenty years from the date of the sale of such utility and franchise on foreclosure."

2. The city's indebtedness and the purposes for which the debt has been incurred; and

3. Such other information as the state fiscal officer may ask for. Thus, whatever be the method of bookkeeping in an individual city, the statements in its annual report will be comparable with the report from every other city in the state.

The state fiscal officer is also clothed with full authority to make or cause to be made at any time a thorough investigation into the financial administration of any city government and the report of his investigation is a public document. Article II., Sec. 15, of the proposed Municipal Corporations Act repeats these constitutional provisions, and under Article II., Sec. 17, of the Act the state financial department may exercise a general supervision over the city's methods of keeping accounts. Article VI. of the Act provides that the City Controller shall have a general supervision and control of all the fiscal affairs of the city, to be exercised in the manner which may be by ordinance prescribed. Thus full opportunity is given for the development of a system of city bookkeeping, accounting, and reporting which will make the experience of each city available to every other.

No time need be spent in describing the system or rather lack of system which has hitherto prevailed in city accounting methods. Neither the city's financial department nor the citizen has been able to learn the city's financial condition with accuracy or to form an intelligent judgment of the quality of services rendered or of the results accomplished for the expenditure of the public money. Yet these are the main purposes of a city's financial accounts and reports. During the past decade the importance of municipal accounts —or rather of municipal accounting, for much more than bookkeeping is involved—has been coming into greater and greater prominence. The National Municipal League was the first organization to take up the matter systematically. It appointed a committee on the subject in 1900 and the investigations and recommendations of that committee have been the initiative of a movement which has now gained such momentum that the entire practicability of establishing methods of accounting that will enable both the citizen and those charged with the conduct of city administration to know what return is received for the expenditure of the public money is no longer doubted. Since 1900 nearly a hundred different cities have demonstrated that better accounting leads to a more intelligent and more economical city administration,[1] and adds greatly to its efficiency.

One need not be a professional accountant in order to state some of the matters which would seem to be essential to any system of city accounts

[1] The Bureau of the Census has for some years been doing effective work in promoting better methods of municipal accounting.

that will enable the citizen to obtain the information to which he is entitled when he examines the financial reports of a city.

Current revenues and expenses.—There should be a complete record of all current revenue as it accrues, whether actually collected or not; for example, taxes, licenses, rents, concessions, franchises, etc., whether actually received in cash or not. Against these should be placed all current expenses, whether actually paid or incurred and not yet paid; for example, salaries, wages, rent, interest, purchases of materials and supplies. These two accounts would show the city's current earnings and expenses during any fiscal period reported upon.

Current assets and liabilities.—There should also be set forth the cash and other current assets in hand, including all uncollected revenues and accounts receivable and all outstanding obligations of the city except its funded debt. These two accounts would enable one to know the city's current assets and liabilities at any given date, for example, at the close of the period reported upon.

Cash receipts and disbursements.—The city's cash receipts during the period reported upon, including receipts from current borrowing (but again omitting the funded debt), and its cash disbursements should be set forth. These would explain the current cash balance reported in the statement of current assets and give information as to the character and the amount of the revenues and other accounts receivable collected and of the expenses and current liabilities paid during the period covered by the report. Cash received during the period but which should have been received prior thereto, and cash paid during the period to discharge obligations incurred prior thereto, should be separately set up in these two accounts.

A report containing the foregoing accounts would enable the citizen to know the city's current revenues and expenses, its current assets and liabilities, and its actual cash receipts and cash expenditures. He could understand the current operating transactions of the city and the status of its current credit.

Appropriations, current borrowings.—Since city officers may lawfully neither spend the city's money nor incur obligations on behalf of the city except pursuant to a duly conferred authority, there should also be accounts showing

1. The appropriations or authorizations to spend and incur liabilities on current account as against the current revenue provisions for meeting them;
2. The authorizations to borrow and to spend and incur liabilities against current borrowings;
3. The receipts and disbursements from current borrowings.

These accounts would inform the citizen as to the city budget and current bond transactions.

Capital account.—There should also be a distinct and separate account kept of the various properties owned by a city and the obligations incurred therefor, and of its permanent funds. This might be called the city's capital account. The capital assets would consist of such things as its sinking fund, permanent improvement funds, real estate, industrial properties and their equipments, e.g., water-works, markets, bridges. The city's capital liabilities would be its funded debt and its capitalized surplus, if any. This account would also be supplemented by a statement of receipts and disbursements. The receipts would be, for example, the amounts realized on flotation of the city's bonds, or on sale of its water-works or any other property; the disbursements would be such matters as payments on account of construction, or the purchase of property, or payments on account of its funded debt.

Cost of administration and degree of administrative efficiency.—A system of city accounts which gave the foregoing information would present the various aspects of the administration of the city as a proprietor. By supplementing these with classified schedules and exhibits of details, the cost of administration and the degree of administrative efficiency would no longer be practically unknown quantities.

The reports of the chief fiscal officer of a city, based on such a system of accounting, could present in clear and intelligible form to every citizen the precise information which he desires to know in order to form a judgment upon the financial conduct of any part of the city's business and upon the results as a whole.

Trust accounts.—One topic remains to be considered. A city government is very often made a trustee of property which is to be devoted to the interest of the community. Each such trust has its own special conditions and their nonobservance may make the city liable. Familiar examples are the gift of funds to a municipal corporation to be used for the purposes of a library, moneys received as security, and deposits on contracts and bids. There should be a separate account of every such trust, setting forth earnings, expenses, assets, liabilities, receipts, and disbursements.

Cities having a population of twenty-five thousand may frame their own charters.

Any city having a population of twenty-five thousand or more may, subject to the constitution and to the general laws of the state and to the special laws as above defined,[1] adopt its own charter and frame of government. A simple method is provided for electing a charter convention to prepare such a charter and frame of government, which, if ratified by the city's voters, supersedes all laws inconsistent therewith and any existing charter and all amendments thereof. A method of making amendments to the charter is also provided.[2]

These "home-made charters," as they are sometimes called, are permitted now in several of

[1] See p. 206 ante.
[2] Articles Fourth and Fifth, Const. Amdt.

our states,[1] and their superiority over the special charters which were the products of state legislative effort has been abundantly established by experience.

SUMMARY.

The City under the Municipal Program.

The city's independence is guaranteed. The state legislature cannot meddle with purely local affairs. Its functions, so far as cities are concerned, are confined to passing laws applicable to all cities or all inhabitants of the state; unless the necessity or propriety of legislative action in the case of a particular city is so clear that a special law receives the affirmative vote of two thirds of all the members of the state legislature and is formally approved by the council of the city, or if disapproved, is within thirty days after such disapproval again passed by a two-thirds vote, which must include three fourths of the members from districts outside of the city concerned.

The city must manage its own affairs. No outside authority can interfere with it.

The city is vested with ample power. It may acquire, hold, manage, and control property; within its corporate limits it has the same powers of taxation as are possessed by the state; it may license and regulate all trades, occupations, and businesses; it is vested with power to perform and render all

[1] See pp. 91–7 ante.

public services, and with all powers of government, subject to the state constitution, and to laws applicable to all cities of the state or to all the inhabitants of the state. It may establish minor courts for the enforcement of its ordinances. The city, not the state legislature, controls the granting of public franchises within the city's limits. It may incur indebtedness up to a certain percentage upon the assessed valuation of the real estate within its limits, but debt incurred for self-supporting undertakings, which also take care of the current interest and of the principal of the debt at maturity, are not included in the constitutional limitation.

Contrast this ample grant of powers with the helpless condition of a city which may not even control its street franchises or the paving of its streets.

The business function of administration and the purely political function of determining the public policy to be administered are intrusted to entirely separate agencies. The former is given wholly to the Mayor and to his appointees, who hold office without fixed terms. The members of the subordinate administrative service must be appointed and promoted upon the merit principle. Prompt dismissal from the service follows failure to perform their duties.

All purely political functions are performed by the Council, subject to the limited veto power of the Mayor.

The Council is the local legislature elected by popular vote on a general ticket from the city at large, one third of the Council being elected at each city election.

There are no gerrymandered election districts. The Council has no patronage to dispense. Its membership is reasonably permanent, and a continuous public policy in important city matters is made possible. The Council may establish any office necessary or expedient for the conduct of the city business or government and may fix its salary and duties. It has absolute initiative in all public matters except as to the annual budget of current expenses, which must be submitted by the Mayor. Any item in the budget may be reduced or omitted by the Council, but it cannot be increased. The Council is the grand committee of the citizens chosen by them for the purpose of determining and regulating all questions of city policy. It chooses the City Controller, who holds office without fixed term, and is the city's chief financial officer, with most important functions.

The Council, if its action is ratified by the citizens, may establish a method of direct legislation, so that the voters may submit, and a majority thereof voting thereon may decide by direct vote upon propositions relative to city matters. In like manner minority or proportional or other method of representation as to elections to elective city offices may be established. On a duly authenticated petition therefor, the questions whether di-

Discussion of Municipal Program 237

rect legislation, or minority, proportional, or other method of representation, shall be established must be submitted to the voters for decision, without previous favorable action by the Council. Under the broad powers granted it, any city may establish the initiative, the referendum, and the recall. The citizens of a city having a population of twenty-five thousand or more may, through a local charter convention elected by themselves, if its action is ratified by them, have a charter and frame of government of their own devising, subject alone to the fundamental provisions of the state constitution.

The members of the Council and the Mayor are the only city officials elected by popular vote, and their election must occur at a different date from state or national elections. The registration of voters, the absolute secrecy of the act of voting are guaranteed. Nominations for Mayor and for members of the Council must be made by petition, and the voter must vote separately for each candidate for whom he desires to vote. The ballot will be simple. The voter will not, confused by the multiplicity of offices and candidates, be forced to rely upon the guidance of the managers of his political party. He votes separately for each candidate for whom he desires to vote.

Such in brief outline is the city under the proposed Municipal Program. It is a representative democracy. The people are the government.

The proposed Constitutional Amendments and General Municipal Corporations Act constituting the Municipal Program submitted by a special committee of the National Municipal League at its meetings in 1898 and 1899 and unanimously adopted by the League in 1899.

TEXT OF THE MUNICIPAL PROGRAM OF THE NATIONAL MUNICIPAL LEAGUE.

CONSTITUTIONAL AMENDMENTS.

ARTICLE FIRST.

Section 1. The right to vote and registration (p. 243).

Sec. 2. Secrecy in voting (p. 243).

Sec. 3. Separation of city elections from state and national elections. Nominations to city office. Method of voting (p. 243).

ARTICLE SECOND.

No private or local bill granting exclusive privileges, immunities, or franchises (p. 244).

ARTICLE THIRD.

Section 1. A city's public places inalienable. Franchises for their use only for limited term. Stated financial reports of the grantee and right of city to inspect grantee's books a condition of their grant (p. 244).

Sec. 2. Limitation of city's power to incur debt and of its tax rate (p. 245).

Sec. 3. City's power to establish direct legislation or minority or proportional or other form of representation as to elections to elective city offices (p. 248).

Sec. 4. Uniform methods of city accounting (p. 249).

Sec. 5. City may establish minor courts (p. 250).

Sec. 6. Organization of cities hereafter created must provide for mayor vested with executive power of city and appointing heads of all city departments except Finance Department; a council; appointments and promotions in administrative service on the merit principle; mayor and members of council only city officers elected by popular vote (p. 250).

Sec. 7. General powers of cities (p. 251).

Sec. 8. Legislatures shall pass a general municipal corporations act (p. 252).

ARTICLE FOURTH.

A city having a population of twenty-five thousand or more may adopt its own charter and frame of government (p. 252).

ARTICLE FIFTH.

PETITIONS (p. 255).

CONSTITUTIONAL AMENDMENTS.

ARTICLE FIRST.

Section 1. *The Right to Vote and Registration.* Laws shall be made for ascertaining by proper proofs the citizens who shall be entitled to vote at popular elections and for the personal registration of voters, which registration shall be completed at least ten days before each election.

Sec. 2. *Secrecy in Voting.* All elections by the citizens shall be by a secret ballot or by such other method as may be prescribed by law, provided that absolute secrecy in voting be preserved. No voter shall disclose at any polling place or within ——— feet thereof how he has voted.

Sec. 3. *City Elections and Nominations. Method of Voting.* Elections of city officers elected by popular vote shall occur at a different date from that of any election by popular vote of officers of the state or national government. Nominations of such city officers shall be by petition, signed by qualified voters of the city concerned. The number of the signatures to such petition shall be determined by the council of the city concerned, but not more than fifty signatures shall be required. Such petition shall be filed in the office of the mayor at least thirty days before the date of the election; provided, however, that in the case of the death or withdrawal of any candidate so nominated such petition may be so filed within a less period than thirty days. The voter must vote separately for each candidate for whom he desires to vote; if the election is by ballot the council of the city shall determine the form of the ballot to be used, but the names of all candidates for the same city office must be printed upon the ballot in alphabetical order under the title of the office.

ARTICLE SECOND.

Private Bills. The legislature shall not pass a private or local bill granting to any private corporation, association, or individual any exclusive privilege, immunity, or franchise whatever.

ARTICLE THIRD.

Section 1. *Streets and Public Places. Franchises.* The rights of every city now existing, or hereafter created within the state, in and to its water front, ferries, wharf property, land under water, public landings, wharves, docks, streets, avenues, parks, bridges, and all other public places, are hereby declared to be inalienable, except by a fourth-fifths vote of all the members elected to the Council approved by the Mayor; and no franchise, lease or right to use the same, either on, through, across, under, or over, and no other franchise granted by a city, to any private corporation, association, or individual, shall be for a longer period than twenty-one years. Such grant and any contract in pursuance thereof may provide that upon the termination of the grant, the plant, as well as the property, if any, of the grantee in the streets, avenues, and other public places shall thereupon, without further or other compensation to the grantee, or upon the payment of a fair valuation thereof, be and become the property of the city; but the grantee shall be entitled to no payment because of any valuation derived from the franchise. Every grant shall specify the mode of determining any valuation therein provided for, and shall make adequate provision by way of forfeiture of the grant, or otherwise, to secure efficiency of public service at reasonable rates, and the maintenance of the property in good order throughout the term of the grant. Every grantee of such franchises or rights to use shall keep books of accounts and make stated quarterly reports to the Financial Department of the city, which shall contain an accurate statement in summarized form and also in detail of all financial receipts from all sources and all expenditures for all purposes, together with a full statement of assets and debts, as well as such other information as to the financial condition of such grantee as said department may require, and said department may inspect and examine, or cause to be inspected and examined, at all reasonable hours, any books of account of such grantee.

Sec. 2. *Municipal Indebtedness. Tax Rate.* No city shall hereafter give any money or property, or loan its money or credit to or in aid of any private individual, association, or corporation; but it may make such provision for the aid and support of its poor as may be authorized by law.

No city shall become indebted for any purpose or in any manner to an amount which, including existing indebtedness, shall exceed―― per centum of the assessed valuation of the real estate within such city subject to taxation as shown by the last preceding assessment for state or city taxes; provided, however, that in determining the limitation of the city's power to incur indebtedness there shall not be included the following classes of indebtedness:―

(1) Certificates of indebtedness or revenue bonds issued in anticipation of the collection of taxes, unless the same be not paid within two years from the date of issue; and all certificates of indebtedness and revenue bonds shall be provided for and payable from the taxes levied for the year in which they are issued, and shall never exceed the amount of such taxes;

(2) Or bonds authorized by the affirmative vote of two thirds of the members of the Council, approved by the Mayor and approved by the affirmative vote of the majority of the qualified voters of the city voting upon the question of their issuance at the next ensuing city election, for the supply of water or for other specific undertaking from which the city will derive a revenue; but from and after a period to be determined by the Council, not exceeding five years from the date of such election, whenever and for so long as such an undertaking fails to produce sufficient revenue to pay all costs of operation and administration (including interest on the city's bonds issued therefor and the cost of insurance against losses by fire, accidents and injuries to persons) and an annual amount sufficient to pay at or before maturity

Constitutional Amendments 247

all bonds issued on account of said undertaking, all such bonds outstanding shall be included in determining the limitation of the city's power to incur indebtedness, unless the principal and interest thereof be payable exclusively from the receipts of such undertaking. The City Controller shall annually report to the Council in detail the amount of the revenue from each such undertaking and whether there is any, and, if so, what deficit in meeting the requirements above set forth.

Provision shall be made at the time of their issue for raising a sum of money by taxation sufficient to pay, as it falls due, the interest upon all city bonds not exclusively payable from the receipts of revenue-producing undertakings, and to pay and discharge the principal thereof within —— [1] years from the date of their issue; but whenever in any year the receipts from any revenue-producing undertaking shall be sufficient to pay the costs of operation and administration as above defined, and the annual amount hereinbefore required, the tax to pay the interest and provide for the principal of the bonds issued for such undertaking shall not be collected, and the same shall be paid from such receipts.

The amount to be raised by tax for city purposes upon real and personal property, or either of them, in addition to providing for the principal and interest of the then outstanding bonded indebtedness shall not in the aggregate exceed in any one year —— per centum of the assessed valuation of the real estate subject to taxation by such city, to be ascertained

[1] This period should not, in the opinion of the committee, exceed thirty years.

as hereinbefore prescribed in respect to the city debt.[1]

Sec. 3. *Direct Legislation. Minority and Proportional Representation.* The Council of any city may, with the consent of the majority of the qualified voters of the city voting thereon at the next ensuing city election taking place not less than —— days thereafter, establish a method of direct legislation so that qualified voters of the city may submit and a majority thereof voting thereon may decide by direct vote propositions relative to city matters, and may also in the same manner establish minority or proportional or other method of representation as to elections to elective city offices. On a petition therefor, filed in the office of the Mayor, signed by qualified voters of the city, equal in number to two per cent. (which shall not be less than one thousand) of those voting at the last preceding city election, a proposition to establish a method of direct legislation, or to establish minority or proportional or other method of representation as to elections to elective city offices, must be submitted to the qualified voters of the city at the next ensuing city election occurring at least —— days thereafter; if a majority of such voters voting upon such proposition are in favor thereof, it shall go at once into effect.

[1] Under this section a city may issue long-term bonds, establish and maintain a sinking fund sufficient to provide for their payment at maturity; or it may have the bonds so drawn that a certain number will mature each year and be paid from the tax as collected. By the latter method the city avoids any risk incident to a sinking fund, the loss of interest on money not invested, any premiums it might pay to buy back its own bonds, and the abuses incident to large accumulations of uninvested money.

Sec. 4. *Uniform Methods of City Accounting.*
Every city shall keep books of account. It shall also make stated financial reports at least as often as once a year to the [1] in accordance with forms and methods prescribed by him, which shall be applicable to all cities within the State; such reports shall be printed as a part of the public documents of the State, and submitted by the [1] to the Legislature at its next regular session. Such reports shall contain an accurate statement in summarized form and also in detail of the financial receipts of the city from all sources, and of the expenditures of the city for all purposes, together with a statement in detail of the debt of said city at the date of said report, and of the purposes for which such debt has been incurred, as well as such other information as may be required by the[1]. Said[1] shall have power by himself, or by some competent person or persons appointed by him, to examine into the affairs of the financial department of any city within the State. On every such examination inquiry shall be made as to the financial condition and resources of the city, and whether the requirements of the constitution and laws have been complied with, and into the methods and accuracy of the city's accounts, and as to such other matters as the said [1] may prescribe. The [1] and every such examiner appointed by him shall have power to administer an oath to any person whose testimony may be required on any such examination, and to compel the appearance, attendance and testimony of any such person for the purpose of any such

[1] State Controller or other officer, or board, which may exercise supervision over municipal finances.

examination, and the production of books and papers. A report of each such examination shall be made, and shall be a matter of public record in the office of said [1].

Sec. 5. *City Courts.* Cities may establish minor courts, which shall have exclusive civil and criminal jurisdiction in the first instance for the enforcement of city ordinances and of penalties for violations thereof. Such courts shall have such further or other jurisdiction as may be conferred by the Legislature, subject to the other provisions of this constitution, but they shall not have any equity jurisdiction, nor any greater jurisdiction in other respects than is conferred upon [2]. No one shall be eligible to appointment as such justice unless he has been [3] for at least five years. Such justices shall be subject to the same liabilities, and their judgments and proceedings may be reviewed in the same manner and to the same extent as is now or may be provided by law in the case of [2] The justices of such courts and, except as otherwise in this constitution provided, all other city judicial officers shall be appointed by the Mayor, and may be removed by him in the same manner as officers in the subordinate administrative service of the city.

Sec. 6. *Municipal Organization.* In the organization of every city hereafter created provision shall be made:

[1] State Controller or other officer, or board which may exercise supervision over municipal finances.

[2] Some lower court recognized as a regularly constituted part of the State's judicial system.

[3] An attorney and counselor-at-law of the State, or some equivalent expression appropriate to the particular State.

For a Council, the members of which shall be elected by the people;

For a Mayor elected by the people.

The Mayor shall be the chief executive officer of the city, and shall appoint and remove all heads of departments in the administrative service of the city, except the head of the Finance Department, who shall be known as the Controller.

The Mayor shall appoint and remove all other officers, agents and employees in the administrative service of the city, and fill all vacancies therein, provided, however, that laborers may be appointed and removed by the heads of departments in which they are employed and that all appointments and promotions in the subordinate administrative service of the city, including laborers, shall be made solely according to fitness, which shall be ascertained, so far as practicable, by examinations that, so far as practicable, shall be open competitive examinations.

All persons in the administrative service of the city, except the Mayor, shall hold their offices without fixed terms.

The Mayor and members of the Council shall be the only city officers, elected by popular vote.

Sec. 7. *General Powers of Cities.* Every city within the State shall be vested with power to acquire, hold, manage, control and dispose of property. Within its corporate limits, it shall have the same powers of taxation as are possessed by the State; it may license and regulate all trades, occupations, and businesses, and shall be vested with power to perform and render all public services, and with all powers of government, subject to such limitations as may be contained in the constitution and laws of the State, applicable either to all the inhabitants of the State or to all the cities of the State, or in such special laws applicable to less than all cities of the State, as may be enacted in the manner hereinafter provided.

Special laws shall require the affirmative vote of two thirds of all the members of the Legislature, and shall not be valid in any city unless they receive the formal approval of its Council within sixty days after the passage thereof by the Legislature, or, within thirty days after disapproval by the Council of the city, shall again be passed by the Legislature by the affirmative vote of two thirds of all the members of the Legislature, which two thirds shall include three fourths of the members of the Legislature, from districts outside of the city or cities to be affected. The failure of the Council of the city to take formal action approving or disapproving a special law shall be deemed a disapproval thereof. Laws repealing such special laws may be passed in the manner provided for the passage of general laws.

Sec. 8. *General Municipal Corporations Act.* The Legislature shall pass a general municipal corporations Act applicable to all the cities in the State which shall, by popular vote, determine to adopt it.

ARTICLE FOURTH.

Power of Cities to Frame Their Own Charters. Subject to the constitution and the laws of the State, applicable to all of the inhabitants or all the cities thereof, and to such special laws as may be passed

Constitutional Amendments

in the manner hereinbefore provided, any city having a population of twenty-five thousand or more may adopt its own charter and frame of government in the following manner:

The Council of said city may, and, on a petition therefor, filed in the office of the Mayor, signed by qualified voters of the city equal in number to two per cent. (which shall not be less than one thousand) of those voting at the last preceding election, must, provide by ordinance for an election to take place not less than —— days nor more than —— days thereafter, upon a proposition for the election of a board of not less than fifteen nor more than —— members, to prepare and propose a charter and frame of government for such city. If such proposition shall receive the affirmative vote of a majority of the qualified voters of the city voting thereon, the Council must, within fifteen days thereafter, provide for the election of such a board within not more than —— days. It shall be the duty of said board to convene upon the ———————— after said election, and thereafter and within —— days to prepare and propose a charter and frame of government for such city, which shall be signed in duplicate by the members thereof or a majority of them, and returned, one copy thereof to the Mayor and the other to the Secretary of State. Such proposed charter and frame of government shall then be published daily in two papers of general circulation in such city for at least twenty days, and within not less than thirty days and not more than sixty days after such publication, shall be submitted to the qualified voters of such city at a special or general municipal election, and the Council of said city shall provide by ordinance for the holding of such special election unless a general municipal election shall be held within the time hereinbefore prescribed.

If a majority of the qualified voters of the city voting thereon shall ratify the same, it shall become the charter and frame of government of such city and the organic law thereof, and supersede and repeal all laws inconsistent therewith and any existing charter and all amendments thereof. A copy of such charter and frame of government duly certified by the proper authorities of such city, setting forth its submission to the legally qualified voters of the city and its ratification by them, shall be made in duplicate, and deposited, one in the office of the Secretary of State and the other among the archives of the city. All courts shall take judicial notice thereof. The charter and frame of government so adopted may be amended at intervals of not less than two years by proposals therefor which the Council of the city may, and when requested by a petition filed in the office of the Mayor, signed by qualified voters of said city equal in number to two per cent. (which shall not be less than one thousand) of those voting at the last preceding city election, must submit at the next city election held at least sixty days after the adoption of the ordinance or the filing of such petition in the office of the Mayor. Each such proposed amendment before it goes into effect must be ratified by a majority of the qualified voters voting thereon, as herein provided for the adoption of the charter and frame of government. In submitting any such proposal any alternative article or proposition may be presented for the choice of the voters, and may be voted on separately without prejudice to others.

ARTICLE FIFTH.

Petitions. After the filing of a petition in accordance with the provisions of the foregoing articles, if the Council of the city neglects or fails to provide by ordinance for an election as hereinbefore directed, then it shall be the duty of the Mayor to order such election, and his order for such purpose, duly signed by him and filed in the archives of the city, shall have the same force and effect as an ordinance for the same purpose.

The petitions mentioned in the foregoing articles need not be one paper, and may be printed or written, but the signatures thereto must be the autograph signatures of the persons whose names purport to be signed. To each signature the house address of the signer must be added, and the signature must be made and acknowledged or proved before an officer authorized by law to take acknowledgment and proof of deeds. The certificate of such officer under his official seal that a signature was so made and acknowledged or proved shall be sufficient proof of the genuineness of the signature for the purposes of these articles.

The signing of another's name, or of a false or fictitious name, to a petition, or the signing of a certificate falsely stating either that a signature was made in the presence of the officer or acknowledged or proved before him, shall be punishable as felonies.

MUNICIPAL CORPORATIONS ACT.

ARTICLE I.

INCORPORATION OF CITIES. PROCEDURE FOR ORGANIZATION OF EXISTING CITIES UNDER THIS ACT AND FOR ANNEXATION OF TERRITORY.

Section 1. Cities, villages, towns, and boroughs heretofore incorporated may organize under this Act (p. 260).

Sec. 2. How a city organized under this Act may annex territory (p. 261).

ARTICLE II.

POWERS OF CITIES.

Section 1. Corporate Powers (p. 263).

Sec. 2. Powers of Ordinance (p. 264).

Sec. 3. Street Powers, Water-works, Buildings, and Sewers (p. 264).

Sec. 4. Wharves, Docks, Harbor, and Ferries (p. 264).

Sec. 5. Markets, Market Places, and Abattoirs (p. 264).

Sec. 6. Charities and Correction (p. 265).

Sec. 7. Fines, Penalties, and Imprisonment (p. 265).

Corporations Act

Sec. 8. Schools, Museums, Libraries, and Other Institutions (p. 265).
Sec. 9. Minor Courts (p. 266).
Sec. 10. Franchises (p. 267).
Sec. 11. Contracts for Labor or Materials Limited to Five Years (p. 268).
Sec. 12. Taxes (p. 269).
Sec. 13. Local Assessments (p. 269).
Sec. 14. Indebtedness and Tax Rate (p. 270).
Sec. 15. City Accounts (p. 273).
Sec. 16. City the Local Authority for Execution of General Laws of the State (p. 274).
Sec. 17. State Supervision of the City's Exercise of its Powers (p. 274).

ARTICLE III.

THE MAYOR.

Section. 1. Mayor's Term of Office (p. 275).
Sec. 2. Filling a Vacancy (p. 275).
Sec. 3. Disability of Mayor (p. 275).
Sec. 4. Removal of Mayor (p. 276).
Sec. 5. Presence of Mayor and Heads of Departments at Council Meetings (p. 276).
Sec. 6. Veto Power of Mayor (p. 276).
Sec. 7. City Budget (p. 277).
Sec. 8. Compensation of Mayor (p. 278).

ARTICLE IV.

THE ADMINISTRATIVE SERVICE OF THE CITY.

Section 1. Appointive Officers (p. 278).
Sec. 2. Civil-service Commissioners (p. 278).

Sec. 3. Civil-service Regulations (p. 279).

Sec. 4. Reports of Civil-service Commissioners (p. 282).

Sec. 5. Duty of Public Officials to Obey Civil-service Regulations (p. 282).

Sec. 6. Civil-service Commissioners to Keep a Roster of the Administrative Service. Payment of Public Employees. Action to Restrain or Recover Illegal Payment of Salaries (p. 283).

Sec. 7. Records of Civil-service Commissioners. Their Duty to Enforce Regulations (p. 284).

Sec. 8. Power of Civil-service Commissioners to Investigate (p. 285).

Secs. 9–15. Specific Prohibitions and Penalties under the Civil-service Provisions of this Act (pp. 287–291).

Sec. 16. Power of Removal (p. 291).

Sec. 17. Power of Mayor to Investigate (p. 292).

ARTICLE V.

THE COUNCIL.

Section 1. Council to Exercise Municipal Powers (p. 292).

Sec. 2. Composition of Council. Members of Council shall Serve without Pay (p. 292).

Sec. 3. Council Judge of the Elections and Qualifications of Its Own Members (p. 293).

Sec. 4. Ineligibility of Councilors (p. 293).

Sec. 5. Council Elects Its Own Officers and Determines Its Own Rules (p. 294).

Sec. 6. Quorum of Council (p. 294).

Sec. 7. Meetings of Council. Proceedings of Council and Sessions of its Committees to be Public.

Corporations Act

Special Requirements as to Publication of Ordinances Granting Franchises (p. 294).

Sec. 8. Council may Establish Municipal Offices (p. 296).

Sec. 9. Council's Powers of Investigation (p. 296).

Sec. 10. Council's Powers to Regulate Assessments, Levy Taxes, and Make Appropriations (p. 296).

Sec. 11. Council may by Ordinance Provide for Direct Legislation or for Minority or Proportional or other Form of Representation in Municipal Elections (p. 297).

ARTICLE VI.

THE CONTROLLER.

Council Elects City Controller. Powers and Duties of Controller (p. 298).

ARTICLE VII.

GENERAL PROVISIONS.

Section 1. Actions by Citizens (p. 301).

Sec. 2. Municipal Elections to Take Place at a Separate Date from State or National Elections (p. 302).

Sec. 3. Nominations for Elective Municipal Office to be Made by Petition at least Thirty Days before Election (p. 303).

Sec. 4. Petitions (p. 303).

ARTICLE I.

THE INCORPORATION OF CITIES.

Section 1. *When City may be Incorporated.*

All cities hereafter created within this State shall be organized under the provisions of this Act.[1] Any city or borough, or any incorporated town or village of —— inhabitants, heretofore incorporated under the Laws of the State, may organize under this Act in the following manner:

On a petition filed in the office of [2] signed by not less than five hundred qualified voters of such corporation, or on the two-thirds vote of the legislative authority of such corporation, there shall be submitted at the next local election,[3] occurring at least thirty days after such filing or vote, the question whether or not the form of organization provided in this Act shall be the form of organization of said corporation, and in case a majority of the qualified voters thereof voting on said question, vote in favor thereof, said city, village, incorporated town, or borough shall

---

[1] A proper method of procedure adapted to the local needs of the State should be provided.

[2] *I. e.* The office where the public records of such corporations are required to be kept, *e.g.*, city clerk's or village clerk's office.

[3] The method of submission must be set forth and should be adapted to the election laws of the particular State.

thereupon be and become a body politic and corporate under the provisions of this Act, provided, however, that the official terms of the officers elected at the next ensuing local election, held in accordance with the provisions of this Act, shall commence, and the terms of all offices and all officers existing under such prior organization shall cease and determine [1] on the first Monday of the month succeeding such local election held under the provisions of this Act. The first election of officers of the new corporation shall take place on the first day for holding local elections, provided by law, which occurs at least sixty days after the adoption of this Act, provided, however, that if there be no such day fixed by law for holding local elections, then such first election [2] shall take place on the last Tuesday of the month following such adoption.

Sec. 2. *Annexation of Territory.*

Any city organized under the provisions of this Act may annex additional territory contiguous and adjacent to the limits of said city in the following manner, and such territory and the inhabitants thereof, when so annexed, shall become a part of said city and subject to the jurisdiction thereof.

Upon a ——————— vote of the Council of the city desiring the annexation of such territory, and a petition filed in the office of the Mayor of the city signed by qualified voters of said territory in number

[1] If this should shorten the term of office contrary to constitutional provisions a different plan would be necessary.

[2] If there is no general law under which such an election can be held, the Act should include appropriate provisions therefor in harmony with the election system of the particular State.

equal to two per cent. of those voting at the last preceding local election, the question whether such territory shall be annexed shall be submitted to the qualified voters residing in said territory at the next general election held therein at least thirty days thereafter, and in case a majority of the qualified voters residing in said territory and voting on said question vote in favor of said annexation, said question shall be submitted to the Legislature of the State, and, in case the Legislature shall vote in favor thereof, the said territory shall thereupon be and become a part of said city, and the public roads and streets thereof become reverts of said city, and the property and liabilities of any therein existing local municipal corporation or corporations shall belong to and be assumed by said city, and the inhabitants of said territory shall become subject in all respects to the jurisdiction of the authorities of said city, and the jurisdiction of any public authority exercised theretofore in said territory shall, so far as it is in conflict with the corporate authority of such city, thereupon cease and determine.

The apportionment of taxation for the payment of the debts of such city and of the local municipal corporation or corporations theretofore existing in such annexed territory shall be adjusted by —— commissioners to be appointed by the judges of the ——— Court, who shall also, in case the territory annexed does not include the entire territory of an existing corporation, equitably apportion the property and liabilities of such corporation between it and such city. Said commissioners shall give public hearings, shall have power to compel the attendance and testimony of witnesses under oath, and the production of books and papers, and shall conduct their proceedings according to the rules that shall be established and published by the judges of said court. Any vacancy occurring in said commission shall be filled by the remaining members. The report of the commissioners, or a majority of them, shall be filed in the office of the clerk of said court, and shall be final and conclusive, unless exceptions are filed thereto within thirty days after filing. In case of exceptions, the court appointing said commission shall have power to overrule the same, and confirm said report, or to set the same aside and refer the matter back to the same, or another commission, when the same proceeding shall be had.

ARTICLE II.

THE POWERS OF CITIES.

Section 1. *Corporate Powers.*

The inhabitants of any city incorporated under this Act are hereby constituted a body politic and corporate which shall have perpetual succession, may use a common seal, sue and be sued, and, for any purpose which it deems necessary or expedient for the public interest, perform and render all public services, and acquire property within or without the city limits by purchase, gift, devise, or by condemnation proceedings, and hold, manage, and control the same.[1]

[1] It should be provided that these proceedings should be conducted in accordance with the general law on the subject if there is one and it is applicable; or that the necessary

Sec. 2. *Powers of Ordinance.*

Every city organized under this Act shall have power to enact and to enforce all ordinances necessary to protect health, life, and property, to prevent and summarily abate and remove nuisances, and to preserve and enforce the good government, order, and security of the city and its inhabitants.

Sec. 3. *Street Powers, Water-works, Buildings, and Sewers.*

Said city shall have power to lay out, establish, open, close, alter, widen, extend, grade, care for, pave, supervise, maintain and improve streets, alleys, sidewalks, squares, parks, public places, and bridges, to vacate the same, and to regulate the use thereof, and to prescribe and regulate the height of buildings adjacent thereto or abutting thereon, and the method and style of construction of the same, to vacate and close private ways, and to construct and maintain water-works and sewers, and to do all things it may deem needful or appropriate to regulate, care for and dispose of sewage, offal, garbage, and other refuse.

Sec. 4. *Wharves, Docks, Harbor, and Ferries.*

The city shall have power to establish, erect, maintain, lease, and regulate wharves and docks, charge wharfage and dockage, regulate the use of the harbor, and establish, lease, regulate, and operate ferries, and charge tolls and ferriage.

Sec. 5. *Markets, Market-places, and Abattoirs.*

The city shall have power to establish, lease,

---

proceedings should be the same as those under which other public or quasi-public corporations may act.

maintain, regulate, and operate markets and market-places and abattoirs.

Sec. 6. *Charities and Correction.*

The city shall have power to establish, maintain, and regulate workhouses, houses of correction, and such other places of incarceration and reformatory institutions, and such hospitals and charitable institutions as it may deem expedient.

Sec. 7. *Fines, Penalties and Imprisonment.*

The city shall have power to enforce obedience to and observance of its ordinances and regulations by ordaining reasonable fines, penalties, and terms of imprisonment.

Sec. 8. *Schools, Museums, Libraries, and Other Institutions.*

The city shall have power to establish and maintain schools, museums, libraries, and such other institutions for the instruction, enlightenment, and welfare of its inhabitants as it may deem appropriate or necessary for the public interest or advantage.

The number, duties, and salaries of teachers and other subordinate officers of such institutions shall be fixed by the officer (or board) in charge of the educational administration of the city.[1]

---

[1] The Committee is of the opinion that the local schools should be under local control subject to a State supervision which compels the local standard to be fully equal to the State standard, and that so far and so rapidly as practicable this result should be accomplished. The Committee is aware, however, that there is a great diversity of practice in the different States, and that on account of the deep popular interest in education there is no branch of the public administration which on the whole has been so successful. It has therefore seemed best to leave the elaboration of the provisions

Sec. 9. *Minor Courts.*

The city shall have the power to establish minor courts for the enforcement of its ordinances, which shall also be vested with the civil and criminal jurisdiction of (justices of the peace)[2]. The justices of such courts shall be men learned in the law, and shall be appointed by the Mayor, and may be removed by him in the same manner as officers in the subordinate administrative service of the city. No one shall be eligible to appointment as such justice unless he has been ———[1] for at least five years. Such justices shall have within the city in which they have been appointed, and in cases where the alleged crime or misdemeanor has been committed within said city, exclusive jurisdiction to issue all warrants, hear and determine all complaints, and to conduct all examinations and trials in criminal cases that may now be had by ——— [2], and shall have the same power and jurisdiction in such criminal cases as ——— [2] now have by law or as may hereafter be conferred upon ——— [2], and shall have exclusive jurisdiction in all cases of violations of such ordinances. Such justices shall be subject to the same liabilities, and their judgments and proceedings may be reviewed in the same manner and to the same extent as now by law provided in the case of [2]

---

of the draft relative to education to be made in accordance with the local conditions of each particular State.

[1] An attorney and counselor-at-law of the State, or some similar expression appropriate to the particular State.

[2] The civil and criminal jurisdiction of justices of the peace is well defined in some States. Where it is not, some other proper officer should be designated. The intention here

Sec. 10. *Street and Other Franchises.*

The rights of the city in and to its water front, ferries, wharf property, land under water, public landings, wharves, docks, streets, avenues, parks, bridges, and all other public places are hereby declared to be inalienable, except by a four-fifths vote of all the members elected to the Council, approved by the Mayor; and no franchise or lease or right to use the same, either on, through, across, under, or over, and no other franchise granted by the city to any private corporation, association, or individual, shall be granted for a longer period than twenty-one years; and, in addition to any other form of compensation, the grantee shall pay annually a sum of money, based in amount upon its gross receipts, to the city. Such grant and any contract in pursuance thereof may provide that, upon the termination of the grant, the plant as well as the property, if any, of the grantee, in the streets, avenues, and other public places shall thereupon, without further or other compensation to the grantee, or upon the payment of a fair valuation thereof, be and become the property of the city, but the grantee shall be entitled to no payment because of any valuation derived from the franchise. Every grant shall specify the mode of determining any valuation therein provided for, and shall make adequate provision by way of forfeiture of the grant

---

is to confer upon municipal judicial officers, to the exclusion of the ordinary minor State judicial officers, such minor civil and criminal jurisdiction as experience has shown should be exercised by magistrates of this class. It is probable that in some States a constitutional amendment would be required in order to enact the provisions of this section into valid law.

or otherwise to secure efficiency of public service at reasonable rates and the maintenance of the property in good order throughout the term of the grant. Every grantee of a franchise from the city rendering a service to be paid for wholly or in part by users of such service shall keep books of account and make stated quarterly reports in writing to the City Controller, which shall contain an accurate statement, in summarized form and also in detail, of all financial receipts from all sources and all expenditures for all purposes, together with a full statement of assets and debts, as well as such other information as to the financial condition of such grantee as the City Controller may require. Such reports shall be public records, and shall be printed as a part of the annual report of the City Controller, and said City Controller may inspect and examine, or cause to be inspected and examined, at all reasonable hours, any books of account of such grantee. Such books of account shall be kept and such reports made in accordance with forms and methods prescribed by the City Controller, which, so far as practicable, shall be uniform for all such grantees.

The city may, if it deems proper, acquire or construct, and may also operate on its own account, and may regulate or prohibit the construction or operation of railroads or other means of transit or transportation and methods for the production or transmission of heat, light, electricity, or other power, in any of their forms, by pipes, wires, or other means.

Sec. 11. *Contracts for Labor and Materials.*

No contract to which the city is a party for serv-

Corporations Act

ices rendered or to be rendered, or for goods or materials furnished or to be furnished, shall be for a longer period than five years.[1]

All contracts except for services rendered shall be made upon specifications, and shall be let in the manner to be prescribed by general ordinance.

In no case shall the contract for any material, machinery or process which or the supply of which, is controlled by one person or company, be let with a contract for work or for other material or machinery.

No contract shall be entered into until after an appropriation has been made therefor, nor in excess of the amount appropriated.

Each contract, before being binding on the city, must be countersigned by the Controller, and charged to the proper appropriation, and whenever the contracts charged to any appropriation equal the amount thereof, no further contracts shall be countersigned by him.

Sec. 12. *Taxes.*

Within its corporate limits the city shall have the same powers of taxation as are possessed by the State. It may license and regulate all trades, occupations, and businesses.

Sec. 13. *Local Assessments.*

The city shall have power to make local improvements by special assessment, or by special taxation, or both, of property adjudged to have received special benefit, or by general taxation; the ascertainment and apportionment of the benefits derived from

[1] The intention of this provision is to prevent the city from entering into any long-term contracts except the issue of long-term bonds.

such local improvements shall be made in accordance with State laws. No improvement to be paid for by special assessment or by special taxation shall be undertaken without the consent of a majority in interest and number of the owners of the property to be taxed or assessed, unless the ordinance therefor shall receive on final passage the affirmative vote of three fourths of all the members of the Council, and be approved by the Mayor after a public hearing of the persons interested, of which due notice shall be given by advertisement in the manner to be prescribed by general ordinance.

Sec. 14. *Indebtedness and Tax Rate.*

The city shall have power to borrow on the credit of the corporation, and issue bonds therefor in such amounts and form, and on such conditions as it shall prescribe, but the credit of the city shall not in any manner be given or loaned to or in aid of any individual, association, or corporation, except that it may make suitable provision for the aid and support of its poor.

No city shall become indebted for any purpose or in any manner to an amount which, including existing indebtedness, shall exceed [1] —— per centum of the assessed valuation of the real estate within such city subject to taxation as shown by the last preceding assessment for State or city taxes; provided, however, that in determining the limitation of the city's power to incur indebtedness there shall not be included the following classes of indebtedness:

[1] The limitation is intended to be the one provided in the State Constitution. If there is no such constitutional provision, it should be fixed somewhere between five and ten per cent., as appears to be proper.

Corporations Act

(1) Certificates of indebtedness or revenue bonds issued in anticipation of the collection of taxes, unless the same be not paid within two years from the date of issue; and all certificates of indebtedness and revenue bonds shall be provided for and payable from the taxes levied for the year in which they are issued, and shall never exceed the amount of such taxes;

(2) Or bonds authorized by the affirmative vote of two thirds of the members of the Council, approved by the Mayor, and approved by the affirmative vote of the majority of the qualified voters of the city voting upon the question of their issuance at the next ensuing city election, for the supply of water or for other specific undertaking from which the city will derive a revenue; but from and after a period to be determined by the Council, not exceeding five years from the date of such election, whenever and for so long as such an undertaking fails to produce sufficient revenue to pay all costs of operation and administration (including interest on the city's bonds issued therefor and the cost of insurance against losses by fire, accidents, and injuries to persons) and an annual amount sufficient to pay at or before maturity all bonds issued on account of said undertaking, all such bonds outstanding shall be included in determining the limitation of the city's power to incur indebtedness, unless the principal and interest thereof be payable exclusively from the receipts of such undertaking. The City Controller shall annually report to the Council in detail the amount of the revenue from each such undertaking and whether there is any and, if so, what deficit in meeting the requirements above set forth.

Provision shall be made at the time of their issue for raising a sum of money, by taxation, sufficient to pay, as it falls due, the interest upon all city bonds not exclusively payable from the receipts of revenue-producing undertakings, and to pay and discharge the principal thereof within ——— [1] years from the date of their issue; but whenever in any year the receipts from any revenue-producing undertaking shall be sufficient to pay the costs of operation and administration as above defined, and the annual amount hereinbefore required, the tax to pay the interest and provide for the principal of the bonds issued for such undertaking shall not be collected, and the same shall be paid from such receipts.

The amount to be raised by tax for city purposes upon real and personal property or either of them, in addition to providing for the principal and interest of the then outstanding bonded indebtedness shall not in the aggregate exceed in any one year —— per centum of the assessed valuation of the real and personal estate subject to taxation by such city, to be ascertained as hereinbefore prescribed in respect to the city debt.[2]

---

[1] This period should not, in the opinion of the committee, exceed thirty years.

[2] Under this section a city may issue long-term bonds, establish and maintain a sinking fund sufficient to provide for their payment at maturity; or it may have the bonds so drawn that a certain number will mature each year and be paid from the tax as collected. By the latter method the city avoids any risk incident to a sinking fund, the loss of interest on money not invested, any premiums it might pay to buy back its own bonds, and the abuses incident to large accumulations of uninvested money.

Sec. 15. *City Accounts.*

Every city shall keep books of account. It shall also make stated financial reports at least as often as once a year to the [1], in accordance with forms and methods prescribed by him, which shall be applicable to all cities within the State. Such reports shall be certified as to their correctness by said [1] or by some competent person or persons appointed by him; they shall be printed as a part of the public documents of the State, and submitted by the [1] to the Legislature at its next regular session. Such reports shall contain an accurate statement, in summarized form and also in detail, of the financial receipts of the city from all sources, and of the expenditures of the city for all purposes, together with a statement in detail of the debt of said city at the date of said report, and of the purposes for which such debt has been incurred, as well as such other information as may be required by [1]. Said [1] shall have power by himself or by some competent person or persons appointed by him, to examine into the affairs of the financial department of any city within this State. On every such examination inquiry shall be made as to the financial condition and resources of the city, and whether the requirements of the constitution and laws have been complied with, and into the methods and accuracy of the city's accounts, and as to such other matters as the said [1] may prescribe. The [1] and every such examiner appointed by him, shall have power to administer an oath to any person whose testimony may be required on

[1] State Controller or other officer, or board which may exercise supervision over municipal finances.

any such examination, and to compel the appearance and attendance of any such person for the purpose of any such investigation and examination, and the production of books and papers. Wilful false swearing in such examinations shall be perjury, and punishable as such. A report of each such examination shall be made, and shall be a matter of public record in the office of said [1]

Sec. 16. *Local Authority for Execution of State Laws.*

Within its corporate limits every city incorporated under the provisions of this Act shall be the local agent of the State government for the enforcement of State laws, to the exclusion of all other public offices, except so far as the contrary may be provided by general law applicable to all the cities of the State.[2]

Sec. 17. *State Supervision.*

Every city incorporated under the provisions of this Act shall, in the exercise of the powers hereby conferred, be subject to the supervision and control of such State administrative boards and officers as may be established for this purpose by general laws applicable to all cities of the State, or may be granted powers of supervision and control, by general act of the Legislature applicable to all cities within the State.[3]

[1] State Controller or other officer, or board which may exercise supervision over municipal finances.

[2] For example, the city, as a corporation, unless there were a general police system applicable to all cities in the State, would be under this section intrusted with the duty of preserving the peace.

[3] For example, the State Board or Superintendent of Education, the State Board of Health, the State Board of Charities.

ARTICLE III.

THE MAYOR.

Section 1. *The Term of Office.*

The chief executive officer of the city shall be a Mayor, who shall be a citizen of the United States, a qualified voter residing within the city limits, and shall hold his office for two years,[1] and until his successor is elected and has qualified.

Sec. 2. *Filling of Vacancy.*

Whenever a vacancy shall occur in the office of the Mayor, the President of the Council shall act as Mayor, and shall possess all the rights and powers of the Mayor, and perform all his duties until the next election, and until his successor is elected and has qualified.

Sec. 3. *Disability of Mayor.*

During the temporary absence or disability of the Mayor the President of the Council shall act as Mayor *pro tempore*, and during such absence or disability

---

[1] Compare Art. V., Sec. 1. The act contemplates a six years' term for a member of the Council, one third of the members going out of office at each biennial election. The Mayor is thus elected at the same time as one third of the Council, and presumably they will be in political accord. The Mayor and one third of the Council have great power when acting together. They will practically control the character of the administration in many important respects.

The biennial elections will enable the citizens effectively to review the conduct of the city administration; and the terms of office fixed by the Act will enable the dates of city elections to occur on the usual election days in November in years alternating with State and National elections, as is done in New York, thus avoiding two elections in the same year.

shall possess the powers of the Mayor and perform his duties, except that he shall not appoint or remove from office any person in the administrative service of the city unless such absence or disability continues for a period of at least —— days.

Sec. 4. *Removal of Mayor*.

In case of misconduct, inability or failure properly to perform his duties, the Mayor may be removed from office by the Governor of the State, after being given an opportunity to be heard in his defense.

The proceedings upon such removal shall be public, and a full detailed statement of the reasons for such removal shall be filed by the Governor in the office of the Secretary of State, and shall be a matter of public record. The decision of the Governor when filed with the reasons therefor shall be final. And the Governor may, pending the investigation, suspend the Mayor for a period of thirty days.

Sec. 5. *Presence of Mayor and Heads of Departments at Council Meetings*.

The Mayor and the heads of the administrative departments of the city shall have the right to be present and participate in the proceedings of the Council, but not to vote. It shall be the duty of the Mayor and of each of the heads of departments to attend the meetings of the Council when specifically requested by the Council, and to answer such questions relative to the affairs of the city under his management as may be put to him by any member of the Council.

Sec. 6. *Veto Power of Mayor*.

Every ordinance or resolution of the Council shall, before it takes effect, be presented duly certified to the Mayor for his approval. The Mayor shall return such ordinance or resolution to the Council within ——— days after receiving it, or at the next meeting of the Council after the expiration of said ——— days; if he approve it, he shall sign it; and if he disapprove it, he shall specify his objections thereto in writing. If he do not return it with such disapproval within the time specified, it shall take effect as if he had approved it. In case of disapproval, the ordinance or resolution may be again passed within ——— days by the votes of at least ———— of all the members elected to the Council. In case an ordinance or resolution of the Council shall appropriate money, the Mayor may approve one or more of the items in such ordinance or resolution, and disapprove the others. In such case those which he shall fail to disapprove shall become effective, and those which he shall disapprove shall become effective only if again passed as above provided.

Sec. 7. *City Budget.*

It shall be the duty of the Mayor from time to time to make such recommendations to the Council as he may deem to be for the welfare of the city, and on the ——— day of ———— in each year to submit to the Council the annual budget of current expenses of the city, any item in which may be reduced or omitted by the Council; but the Council shall not increase any item in nor the total of said budget.[1]

[1] The purpose of this provision is to give the Mayor, who is the head of the administrative service, the power to make up the annual budget of current expenses, subject to the power of the Council to reduce but not to increase the pro-

Sec. 8. *Compensation of Mayor.*

The Mayor of any city incorporated under this Act may be paid a salary, the amount of which shall be fixed by the Council; but no Council shall change the salary of any Mayor after his election.

ARTICLE IV.

THE ADMINISTRATIVE SERVICE OF THE CITY.

Section 1. *Appointive Officers.*

The Mayor shall have power to appoint all heads of departments in the administrative service of the city, except the City Controller. Subject to the restrictions and limitations hereinafter contained, the Mayor shall have power to appoint all officers and employees in the subordinate administrative service of the city, and to fill all vacancies therein, except that laborers may be appointed and removed by the heads of departments in which they are employed.

Sec. 2. *Civil-service Commissioners.*

The Mayor shall appoint three or more suitable persons to be known as Municipal Civil-service Commissioners, who shall prescribe, amend, and enforce regulations for appointment to, and promotion in, and for examinations in the administrative service of the city, including the appointment and employment of laborers therein. Such Commissioners shall not hold any other paid position in the public

---

posed appropriations. Appropriations for other purposes than current expenses and for emergencies are provided for in Art. V., Sec. 10.

service. The regulations and amendments thereof made under the authority of this Act, or a copy certified by the Secretary of said Commissioners, shall be received in evidence in all courts and places.

Sec. 3. *Civil-service Regulations.*

Such regulations shall, among other things, provide:

1. For the classification of the offices, places, and employments in the administrative service of the city.

Such classification shall be based on the respective duties and functions of the offices and positions affected, and on the amounts of the salary or other compensation attached thereto, and shall be arranged so as to permit the grading of offices and positions like in character in groups and subdivisions, and so as to permit the filling of offices and positions in the higher grades, so far as practicable, through promotion.

2. For examinations, wherever practicable, to ascertain the fitness of all applicants for appointment to the administrative service of said city. Public notice shall be given of all examinations, and the Commissioners shall adopt reasonable rules for permitting the presence of representatives of the press.

No question in any examination under the regulations established as aforesaid shall relate to political or religious opinions, affiliations or services, and no appointment or selection to or removal from any office or employment within the scope of the regulations established as aforesaid, and no transfer, promotion, reduction, reward, or punishment shall be in any manner affected or influenced by such opinions, affiliations, or services. Such examinations shall be practical in their character, and shall relate to those matters which will fairly test the relative fitness of the persons examined to discharge the duties of the positions to which they seek to be appointed. Such examinations, save in the case of applicants for employment as ordinary (not skilled) laborers, shall be open, competitive examinations, except where, after due efforts by previous public advertisement or other effort in case of extraordinary emergency, competition is found not to be practicable. The examination of applicants for employment as ordinary laborers shall relate to their capacity for labor and their habits as to industry and sobriety, and shall be accompanied by such physical examination and tests, competitive or otherwise, as the Commission, in its discretion, may determine.

3. For the filling of vacancies in the offices, places, and employments in the administrative service of the city which are subject to competitive examination by selection from a number not exceeding three graded highest as the result of such examination; and for the selection of laborers, from among those found qualified, on the basis of priority of application.

In the absence of an appropriate eligible list, from which appoinments are to be made, and pending the preparation of such list, any office, place, or employment subject to competitive examination may be filled temporarily without such examination, but not for a longer period than thirty days. No person shall be appointed or employed under any title not appropriate to the duties to be performed, and no person shall be transferred to, or assigned to perform the duties of, any position subject to competitive examination, unless he shall have been appointed to the position from which transfer is made as the result of an open, competitive examination equivalent to that required for the position to be filled, or unless he shall have served with fidelity for at least five years in a similar position. A copy of each list of eligibles, with their respective grades, shall be accessible to each person whose name appears upon such list.

4. For a period of probation not exceeding three months before an appointment or employment is made permanent.

5. For promotion from the lower grades to the higher based on merit and competition and seniority of service.

An increase in the salary or other compensation of any person holding an office, place, or employment within the scope of the rules in force hereunder shall be deemed a promotion.

No public officer or employee shall be deemed or held to be excluded from the operation of this Act, or from competitive examination, nor shall competitive examination be deemed or held to be impracticable, on the ground or for the reason that any office, place, or employment or any of the duties thereof, is confidential in character, or by reason of the fact that fiduciary responsibility is involved, or by reason of the fact that any bond or security is or shall be required of the appointee; provided, however, that in advance of any competitive examination for any office, place, or employment, the appointing officer may, where otherwise permitted by law, publicly prescribe the amount and the necessary details of the bond or security which shall be required to be given by any such appointee, and provided further that any surety company, the bonds of which are accepted by a Justice of ———— Court, shall be a sufficient surety on any such bond.

Sec. 4. *Reports of Civil-service Commissioners.*

The Municipal Civil-service Commissioners shall have authority to employ a secretary and such other assistance as may be necessary for the performance of their duties as provided in this Act, and shall make reports from time to time to the Mayor, whenever said Mayor may request, of the manner in which the regulations hereinbefore provided for have been and are administered, and the result of their administration in such city, and of such other matters as said Mayor may require, and annually, and on or before the —— day of ——— in each year, shall make a report to the Mayor; and it shall be the duty of the Mayor to transmit either these reports, or a sufficient abstract or summary thereof to give full and clear information as to their contents, to the Council annually on or before the —— day of ——.

Sec. 5. *Duty of Officers to Obey Regulations.*

It shall be the duty of all persons in the public service of the city to conform to and comply with said regulations and any modifications thereof made pursuant to the authority of this Act, and to aid and facilitate in all proper ways the enforcement of said regulations and any modifications thereof, and the holding of all examinations which may be required under the authority of this Act by said regulations. Proper provision shall be made in the annual budget for all the expenses of the Municipal Civil-service Commissioners.

Sec. 6. *Roster of Administrative Service. Payment of Public Employees. Action to Restrain or Recover Illegal Payments.*

It shall be the duty of said Civil-service Commissioners to prepare, continue, and keep in their office a complete roster of all persons other than ordinary laborers in the public service of the city. This roster shall be open to inspection at all reasonable hours. It shall show in reference to each of said persons his name, the date of his appointment to or employment in such service, his salary or compensation, the title of the place or office he holds, the nature of the duties thereof, and the date of any termination of such service. It shall be the duty of all officers of the city to give to the Civil-service Commissioners all the information which may be reasonably requested, or which the regulations established by the Civil-service Commissioners may require in aid of the preparation or continuance of said roster, and so far as practicable said roster shall state whether any and what persons are holding any and what offices or places aforesaid in violation of this act or of any regulations made thereunder. Said Civil-service Commissioners shall have access to all public records and papers, the examination of which will aid the discharge of their duty in connection with said roster. It shall be the duty of said Commissioners to certify to the City Controller the name of each person appointed or employed in the public service of the city (ordinary laborers excepted), stating in each case the title or character of the office or employment, the date of the commencement of service by virtue thereof, and the salary or other compensation paid, and also, as far as practicable, the name of each person employed in violation of this Act or of the regulations established thereunder, and to certify to the said Controller in like manner every change occurring in any office or employment of the public service of the city forthwith on the occurrence of the change. No officer of said city whose duty it is to sign or countersign warrants shall draw, sign, countersign, or issue, or authorize the drawing, signing, or issuing of any warrant or order on any disbursing officer of the city for the payment of salary or compensation to any person in its public service required to be so certified as aforesaid who is not so certified as having been appointed or employed in pursuance of this Act or of the regulations in force thereunder. Any person entitled to be certified as aforesaid may maintain a proceeding by mandamus to compel the issue of such certificate. Any sums paid contrary to the provisions of this section may be recovered from any disbursing officer of the city paying the same or signing, countersigning, drawing, or issuing, or authorizing the drawing, signing, or issuing of any warrant or order for the payment thereof, and from the sureties on his official bond in an action in the ——— Court. All moneys recovered in any action brought under the provisions of this section must, when collected, after paying all expenses of such action, be paid into the city treasury.

Sec. 7. *Records of Civil-service Commissioners. Their Duty to enforce Regulations.*

The said Commissioners shall keep records of their

proceedings; they shall make regulations for and have control of such applications, registrations, certifications, and examinations as are or may be provided for under this Act and the regulations established under their authority, and shall cause a record thereof to be kept and of the markings and gradings upon such examinations; and all recommendations of applicants for office or employment received by them, or by any officer having authority to make appointments or select employees in the public service as classified by said Commissioners, shall be kept and preserved by said Commissioners. And all such records and regulations shall, subject to such reasonable regulations as may be made by said Commissioners, be open to public inspection.

It shall be the duty of the Civil-service Commissioners to supervise the execution of this law and the regulations thereunder, and to see that the same be enforced, and they shall be responsible for correcting all abuses and irregularities occurring in the administration of said law and the regulations thereunder, and shall investigate all complaints in respect of such abuses and irregularities made to them. They shall supervise the examinations thereunder and the markings and gradings upon such examinations, and shall keep themselves well informed concerning the same in all parts of the public service to the end that such examinations, markings, and gradings shall be as uniform and just as possible.

Sec. 8. *Power of Civil-service Commissioners to Investigate.*

A majority of said Commissioners shall constitute a

quorum. The said Commissioners may make investigations concering the facts in respect to the execution of this Act, and of the regulations established under its authority, and in the course of such investigations each Commissioner and their secretary and such other assistant as they may designate shall have the power to administer oaths. Said Commissioners shall have power, for the purposes provided for in this Act, to examine into books and records, compel the production of books and papers, subpoena witnesses, administer oaths to them, and compel their attendance and examination, as though such subpoena had issued from a court of record of this State; and witnesses and officers to subpoena and secure the attendance of witnesses before the said Commissioners, shall be entitled to the same fees as are allowed to witnesses in civil cases in courts of record. Such fees need not be prepaid, but the proper disbursing officer of the city shall pay the amount thereof when the same shall have been certified by the president of the Commissioners, and duly proved by affidavit or otherwise to the satisfaction of the said officer; and all officers in the public service and their deputies, clerks, subordinates, and employees shall afford the said Commissioners all reasonable facilities in conducting their inquiries specified in this Act, and give inspection to said Commissioners of all books, papers, and documents belonging or in anywise appertaining to their respective offices, and also shall produce said books and papers, and shall attend and testify when required to do so by said Commissioners. Wilful false swearing in such investigations and examinations shall be perjury and punishable as such.

Secs. 9–15. *Specific Prohibitions and Penalties under the Civil-service Provisions of the Act.*

Sec. 9. Any commissioner, examiner, or any other person who shall wilfully or corruptly, by himself or in co-operation with one or more persons, defeat, deceive, or obstruct any person in respect to his or her right to examination or registration according to any regulations prescribed pursuant to the provisions of this Act, or who shall, wilfully or corruptly, falsely mark, grade, estimate, or report upon the examination or proper standing of any person examined, registered, or certified according to any regulations prescribed pursuant to the provisions of this Act, or aid in so doing, or who shall wilfully or corruptly make any false representations concerning the same, or concerning the person examined, registered, or certified, or who shall wilfully or corruptly furnish to any person any special or secret information for the purpose of either improving or injuring the prospects or chances of any person so examined, registered, or certified, or to be examined, registered, or certified, or who shall personate any other person, or permit or aid in any manner any other person to personate him, in connection with any examination or registration or application or request to be examined or registered, shall for each offense be deemed guilty of a misdemeanor.

Sec. 10. No person in the national public service or the public service of the State or any civil division thereof, including counties, cities, towns, villages, and boroughs, shall, directly or indirectly, use his authority or official influence to compel or induce any person in the public service of a city to pay or to promise to pay any political assessment, subscription, or contribution. Every person who may have charge or control in any building, office, or room, occupied for any purpose of said public service of a city is hereby authorized to prohibit the entry of any person into the same, and he shall not knowingly permit any person to enter the same for the purpose of therein making, collecting, receiving, or giving notice of any political assessment, subscription, or contribution, and no person shall enter or remain in any said office, building, or room, or send or direct any letter or other writing thereto for the purpose of giving notice of, demanding, or collecting, nor shall any person therein give notice of, demand, collect, or receive any such assessment, subscription, or contribution; and no person shall prepare or make out, or take part in preparing or making out, any political assessment, subscription, or contribution with the intent that the same shall be sent or presented to, or collected from any person in the public service of the city, and no person shall knowingly send or present any political assessment, subscription, or contribution to or request its payment by any person in said public service.

Any person who shall be guilty of violating any provision of this section shall be deemed guilty of a misdemeanor.

Sec. 11. Whoever, being a public officer or being in nomination for, or while seeking a nomination or appointment for, any public office, shall use, or promise to use, whether directly or indirectly, any official authority or influence (whether then possessed or merely anticipated) in the way of conferring upon any person, or in order to secure or aid any person to secure any office or appointment in the public service, or any nomination, confirmation, or promotion, or increase of salary, upon the consideration or condition that the vote or political influence or action of the last-named person or any other shall be given or used in behalf of any candidate, officer, or political party or association, or upon any other corrupt condition or consideration, shall be deemed guilty of bribery or an attempt at bribery. And whoever, being a public officer or employee, or having or claiming to have any authority or influence for or affecting the nomination, public employment, confirmation, promotion, removal or increase or decrease of salary of any public officer or employee, shall corruptly use, or promise or threaten to use, any such authority or influence, directly or indirectly, in order to coerce or persuade the vote or political action of any citizen, or the removal, discharge, or promotion of any public officer or public employee, or upon any other corrupt consideration, shall be also guilty of bribery, or an attempt at bribery. And every person found guilty of such bribery, or an attempt to commit the same, as aforesaid, shall, upon conviction thereof, be liable to be punished by a fine of not less than one hundred dollars or more than three thousand dollars, or to be imprisoned not less than ten days or more than two years, or to both said fine and said imprisonment, in the discretion of the court. If the person convicted be a public officer he shall, in addition to any other punishment imposed, be deprived of his office and be ineligible to any public office or employment for —— years thereafter. The phrase "public officer" shall be held to include all public officials in this State, whether paid directly or indirectly from the public treasury of the State, or from that of any civil division thereof, including counties, cities, towns, villages, and boroughs, and whether by fees or otherwise; and the phrase "public employee" shall be held to include every person not being an officer who is paid from any said treasury.

Sec. 12. No recommendation of any person who shall apply for office or place, or for examination or registration under the provisions of this Act, or the regulations established under the authority thereof, except as to residence and as to character, and in the case of former employers as to the abilities, when said recommendation as to character and abilities is specifically required by said regulations, shall be given to or considered by any person concerned in making any examination, registration, appointment, or promotion under this Act or under the regulations established under the authority thereof. No recommendation or question under the authority of this Act shall relate to the political or religious opinions or affiliations of any person whomsoever.

Sec. 13. No person in the service of the city is for that reason under any obligation to contribute to any political fund or to render any political service, and no person shall be removed, reduced in grade or salary, or otherwise prejudiced for refusing to do so. No person in the service of the city shall discharge, or promote, or degrade, or in any manner change the official rank or compensation of any other person in said service, or promise or threaten to do so for giving or withholding, or neglecting to make any contribution of money or service or any other valuable thing for any political purpose. No person in said service shall use his official authority or influence to coerce the political action of any person or body, or to affect or interfere with any nomination, appointment, or election to public office.

Sec. 14. Whoever, after a regulation has been duly established according to the provisions of this Act, makes an appointment to office in the public service of the city or selects a person for employment therein contrary to the provisions of such regulation, or wilfully refuses or neglects otherwise to comply with, or conform to, the provisions of this Act, or violates any of such provisions, shall be guilty of a misdemeanor.

Sec. 15. Misdemeanors under the provisions of this Act shall be punishable by a fine of not less than ———— ———— dollars nor more than ———————— dollars, or by imprisonment for not longer than————————, or by both such fine and imprisonment.

Sec. 16. *Power of Removal.*

No officer or employee in the administrative service of the city shall be removed, reduced in grade or salary, or transferred because of the religious or political beliefs or opinions of such officer or employee; nor shall any official in the administrative service of the city be removed, reduced, or transferred without first having received a written statement setting forth in detail the reasons therefor; a duplicate copy of such statement shall be filed in the office of the Civil-service Commissioners, and at the option of the official who shall have been removed, reduced, or transferred, such statement of reasons, together with the reply thereto made by the officer removed, shall be made a matter of public record in the archives of the city. Subject to the foregoing provisions of this Act, all persons in the administrative service of the city shall hold their offices without fixed terms and subject to the pleasure of the Mayor.

Sec. 17. *Mayor May Investigate.*

The Mayor may at any time, with or without notice, investigate in person or by agent or agents appointed by him for this purpose, the affairs of any department of the city government, and the official acts and conduct of any official in the administrative service of the city. For the purpose of ascertaining facts in connection with these examinations, the Mayor or the agent or agents so appointed by him shall have full power to compel the attendance and testimony of witnesses, to administer oaths, and to examine such persons as they shall deem necessary, and to compel the production of books and papers. Wilful false swearing in such investigations and examinations shall be perjury, and punishable as such.

ARTICLE V.

THE COUNCIL.

Section 1. *Council to Exercise Municipal Powers.*

There shall be a City Council which shall have full power and authority, except as otherwise provided, to exercise all powers conferred upon the city, subject to the veto of the Mayor, as hereinbefore provided.

Sec. 2. *Composition of the Council.*

The Council shall consist of [1] —— members, who

[1] At least nine and not more than fifty, the precise number being determined by the local conditions of each State.

shall serve without pay, one third of whom shall be elected at each municipal election. The members of the Council shall be elected on a general ticket from the city at large, and shall serve from —— after their election. The members of the first Council elected under the provisions of this Act shall be divided by lot into three classes, as nearly equal in number as may be, to hold office respectively for two, four, and six years, and thereafter at each municipal election there shall be elected members of the Council to take the place of outgoing members for a term of six years, and to fill for the unexpired term any vacancies that may have occurred in the respective classes.[1] Outgoing members of the Council shall be eligible for re-election.

Sec. 3. *The Council to be Judge of Election and Qualifications of its own Members.*

The Council shall be the judge of the election and qualifications of its own members, subject to review by the courts.

Sec. 4. *Ineligibility of Councilors.*

No member of the Council shall hold any other public office or hold any office or employment the compensation for which is paid out of public moneys; or be elected or appointed to any office created or the compensation of which is increased by the Council

[1] In States where the conditions make it practicable to hold two elections at different times in the same year without subordinating local questions to issues of national or State politics, and the interest of the voters in public affairs can be sufficiently aroused to permit two vigorous political campaigns in the same year, the term of a member of the Council could be made three years, one third of the Council being elected each year.

while he was a member thereof, until one year after the expiration of the term for which he was elected; or be interested directly or indirectly in any contract with the city; or be in the employ of any person having any contract with the city, or of any grantee of a franchise granted by the city.

Sec. 5. *The Council Shall Elect Its Own Officers and Determine Its Own Rules.*

The Council shall elect its own officers; determine its own rules of procedure; may punish its members for disorderly conduct, and compel the attendance of members, and, with the concurrence of —— of the members elected, expel a member. Any member who shall have been convicted of bribery shall thereby forfeit his office.

Sec. 6. *Quorum of the Council.*

A majority of the members of the Council elected shall constitute a quorum to do business, but a smaller number may adjourn from time to time, and may compel the attendance of absentees under such penalties as may be prescribed by ordinance.

Sec. 7. *Council Meetings.*

The Council may prescribe by ordinance the time and place of its meetings and the manner in which special meetings thereof may be called. But the Mayor may call a special meeting of the Council at any time by previous written notice mailed to the post-office address of each member of the Council at least twenty-four hours before such special meeting. The Council shall elect one of its own number as president, shall sit with open doors, shall keep a journal of its own proceedings, which shall be public and printed. All sessions of committees of the

Council shall be public. The Council shall act only by ordinance or resolution, and all ordinances or resolutions, except ordinances making appropriations, shall be confined to one subject, which shall be clearly expressed in the title, and ordinances making appropriations shall be confined to the subject of appropriations. The ayes and nays shall be taken upon the passage of all ordinances or resolutions and entered upon the journal of its proceedings; and every ordinance or resolution shall require on final passage the affirmative votes of a majority of all the members.

No ordinance or resolution shall be passed finally on the day it is introduced, except in case of public emergency, and then only when requested by the Mayor and approved by the affirmative votes of three fourths of all the members of the Council.

Except in case of such public emergency, each ordinance when introduced shall be referred to a committee and printed for the use of members, and shall not be subsequently so altered or amended as to change its original purpose. It shall be reported to the Council at the next regular meeting thereof, unless another date be designated by the Council when the reference is made, or at a subsequent meeting thereof.

Before any grant of a franchise shall be made, the proposed specific grant embodied in the form of an ordinance, with all the terms and conditions, including the provisions as to rates, fares, and charges, shall be published at the expense of the applicant for the franchise at least twice in each of two newspapers designated by the Mayor having a general circulation in the city. Such publication shall take place at least —— days before the final vote upon such ordinance, and such ordinance shall require the affirmative vote of at least —————— of all the members of the Council.

Sec. 8. *Council May Establish Municipal Offices.*

The Council, except as herein before provided, shall have power to establish any office that may in its opinion be necessary or expedient for the conduct of the city's business or government, and may fix its salary and duties; but no city official shall be elected by popular vote except the Mayor and the members of the Council. The incumbents of all offices established by the Council shall be appointed by the Mayor, as herein provided, except that the Council may elect its own officers.

Sec. 9. *The Council's Powers of Investigation.*

The Council, or a committee of the Council duly authorized by it may investigate any department of the city government and the official acts and conduct of any city officer; and for the purpose of ascertaining facts in connection with such investigation, shall have full power to compel the attendance and testimony of witnesses, to administer oaths, and to examine such persons as it may deem necessary, and to compel the production of books and documents. Wilful false swearing in such investigations and examinations shall be perjury and punishable as such.

Sec. 10. *Council's Power to Regulate Assessments, Levy Taxes and Make Appropriations.*

The Council shall provide by general ordinance for the appraisement and assessment of all property subject to taxation and for the collection and enforcement of taxes and assessments and for penalties for non-payment thereof. Such taxes, assessments and penalties shall be a lien upon the property affected thereby until paid.

All taxes shall be levied and appropriations made annually, not more than sixty days nor less than thirty days before the date for holding municipal elections, except such taxes as may be levied and appropriations as may be made to provide for debts already incurred or continuing contracts already entered into. And except, also, in cases of emergency, when on a certificate signed by the Mayor and Controller that such emergency exists, a special appropriation may be made to meet the same.

Subject to the foregoing, and other provisions of this Act, the Council shall have the power to appropriate all money necessary to provide for the expenses of the city government, to make special appropriations, and to transfer to a different appropriation the unexpended balance of an appropriation already made, and not needed for the completion of the work for which such appropriation was originally made.

Sec. 11. *Direct Legislation; Minority or Proportional or Other Form of Representation in City Elections.*

The Council of any city now existing or hereafter created within the State may, with the consent of a majority of the qualified voters of the city voting thereon at the next ensuing city election taking place not less than —— days thereafter, establish a method of direct legislation so that qualified voters of the city may submit and a majority thereof voting thereon may decide by direct vote propositions relative to city matters, and may also in the same manner establish minority or proportional or other method of representation as to elections to elective city offices.

On a petition therefor, filed in the office of the Mayor, signed by qualified voters of the city equal in number to two per cent. (which shall not be less than one thousand) of those voting at the last preceding city election, a proposition to establish a method of direct legislation or to establish minority or proportional or other method of representation as to elections to elective city offices, must be submitted to the qualified voters of the city at the next ensuing city election occurring at least —— days thereafter; if a majority of such voters voting upon such proposition are in favor thereof, such proposition shall go at once into effect.

ARTICLE VI.

THE CONTROLLER.

The Council to Elect City Controller; his Powers and Duties.

The Council shall elect, and may by resolution remove, a Controller who shall have a general supervision and control of all the fiscal affairs of the city, to be exercised in the manner which may be by ordinance prescribed. It shall be his duty to keep the books of account and to make the financial reports provided for in Article II., Section 15, of this Act. His books shall also exhibit accurate and detailed statements of all moneys received and expended for account of the city by all city officers and other persons, and of the property owned by the city and the income derived therefrom. He shall also keep separate accounts of each appropriation, and of the dates, purpose, and manner of each payment therefrom.

The Controller shall keep a separate record for each grantee of a franchise from the city rendering a service to be paid for wholly or in part by users of such service, which record shall show in the case of each such grantee:—

1. The true and entire cost of construction, of equipment, of maintenance, and of the administration and operation thereof; the amount of stock issued if any; the amount of cash paid in, the number and par value of shares, the amount and character of indebtedness, if any; the rate of taxes, the dividends declared; the character and amount of all fixed charges; the allowance, if any, for interest, for wear and tear or depreciation, all amounts and sources of income;

2. The amount collected annually from the city treasury and the character and extent of the service rendered therefor to the city;

3. The amount collected annually from other users of the service and the character and extent of the service rendered therefor to them. Such books of record shall be open to public examination at any time during the business hours of the Controller's office.

The Controller shall examine and audit all bills, claims, and demands against the city, and shall promptly report in writing to the Mayor and to the Council any default or delinquency he may discover in the accounts of any city officer.

The Controller may require any person presenting for settlement an account or claim for any cause whatever against the city to be sworn or affirmed before him, touching such account or claim, and when so sworn or affirmed, to answer orally as to any facts relative to the justness of such account or claim. Wilful false swearing before him shall be perjury, and punishable as such. He shall settle and adjust all claims in favor of or against the city, and all accounts in which the city is concerned as debtor or creditor, but in adjusting and settling such claims, he shall, so far as practicable, be governed by the rules of law and principles of equity which prevail in courts of justice. The power hereby given to settle and adjust such claims shall not be construed to give such settlement and adjustment the binding effect of a judgment or decree, nor to authorize the Controller to dispute the amount or payment of any salary established by or under the authority of any officer or department authorized to establish the same, because of failure in the due performance of his duties by such officer, except when necessary to prevent fraud.

No payment of city funds shall be made except upon draft or warrant countersigned by the Controller, who shall not countersign any such draft or warrant until he has examined and audited the claim, and found the same justly and legally due and payable, and that the payment has been legally authorized, and the money therefor has been duly appropriated, and that the appropriation has not been exhausted.

The City Controller shall, on or before the 15th day of January, in each year, prepare and transmit to the City Council a report of the financial transactions of the city during the calendar year ending the 31st day of December [1] next preceding, and of its financial condition on said 31st day of December. The report shall contain an accurate statement, in summarized form, and also in detail, of the financial receipts of the city from all sources, and of the expenditures of the city for all purposes, together with a detailed statement of the debt of said city, of the purposes for which such debt had been incurred, and of the property of said city, and of the accounts of the city with grantees of franchises.

ARTICLE VII.

GENERAL PROVISIONS.

Section 1. *Actions by Citizens.*

Any ——————— or more citizens who are householders of said city may maintain an action in the proper court to restrain the execution of any illegal, unauthorized, or fraudulent contract or agreement on behalf of said city, and to restrain any disbursing officer of said city from paying any illegal, unauthorized, or fraudulent bills, claims, or demands against said city, or any salaries or compensation to any person in its administrative service whose appointment has not been made in pursuance of the provisions of law and the regulations in force thereunder. And in case any such illegal, unauthorized, or fraudulent bills, claims, or demands, or any such salary or compensation shall have been paid, such citizens may maintain

[1] This section assumes December 31st to be the end of the city's fiscal year.

an action in the name of said city against the officer making such payment, and the party receiving the same, or either, or both, to recover the amount so paid, and such amount, after deducting all expenses of the action, shall be paid into the city treasury, provided, however, that the court may require such citizens to give security to indemnify the city against costs, unless the court shall decide that there was reasonable cause for bringing the action. The right of any householder of the city to bring an action to restrain the payment of compensation to any person appointed to or holding any office, place, or employment in violation of any of the provisions of this Act, shall not be limited or denied by reason of the fact that said office, place, or employment shall have been classified as, or determined to be, not subject to competitive examination; provided, however, that any judgment or injunction granted or made in any such action shall be prospective only, and shall not affect payments already made or due to such persons by the proper disbursing officers.

In case of any unsatisfied judgment or any suit or process of law against said city, any ———— or more citizens who are householders of said city shall, upon petition, accompanied by affidavit that they believe that injustice will be done to said city in said suit or judgment, be permitted to intervene and inquire into the validity of such judgment or defend said suit or action, as fully and completely as the officers of said city would by law have the right to do.

Sec. 2. *Separate City Elections.*[1]

[1] No election for any city office should be held at a time coinciding with the time for holding State or national elections.

Sec. 3. *Nominations*.

Candidates for elective city offices shall be nominated by petition signed by qualified voters of the city. The number of the signatures to such petition shall be determined by the Council of the city, but no more than fifty signatures shall be required. Such petition shall be filed in the office of the Mayor at least thirty days before the date of the election; provided, however, that in the case of the death or withdrawal of any candidate so nominated, such petition may be so filed within a less period than thirty days. The voter must vote separately for each candidate for whom he desires to vote; if the election is by ballot the Council of the city shall determine the form of ballot to be used, but the names of all candidates for the same office must be printed upon the ballot in alphabetical order under the title of such office.

Sec. 4. *Petitions*.

The petitions provided for in this Act need not be one paper, and may be printed or written, but the signatures thereto must be the autograph signatures of the persons whose names purport to be signed. To each signature the house address of the signer must be added, and the signature must be made and acknowledged or proved before an officer authorized by law to take acknowledgment and proof of deeds. The certificate of such officer under his official seal that a signature was so made and acknowledged or proved shall be sufficient proof of the genuineness of the signature for the purposes of this Act. The signing of

---

Proper provisions to accomplish this result should be drawn in harmony with the general system of holding elections in the particular State.

another's name, or of a false or fictitious name, to a petition or the signing of a certificate falsely stating either that a signature was made in the presence of the officer or acknowledged or approved before him, shall be punishable as felonies.

INDEX

PAGE

Accounts, Municipal
    (see Index to Municipal Program)
Administrative or "Business" Side of Government
    (see also Administrative System,
        Government is Government)
    Necessary to any government . . . 4, 9
    Involves no divisive partisan issues . . 4, 5
    Distinction between, and political side
        Growing appreciation of . . 61 *et seq.*
        (see also Political Side)
Administrative System, Municipal
    (see also English Municipal System
        Merit Principle
        Administrative Side)
    Should be controlled by the city . . . 128
    Should be framed by the city 189
    No state interference 153–5
    Evils of state interference . . . 135–7
    (see State Supervision)
    Administrative Service
        Politics in
            (see Merit Principle)
            Not necessary 4, 5, 8
            Illustrated by analogy of private
                business 5, 6
            Demoralizes service . . 6, 8, 9, 158–9
            Must be prevented 6, 8, 9
        Personnel of
            Should be efficient . . . 4, 5, 8, 9
            Political opinions unimportant 4, 5, 8, 10
            Should be appointed, not elected 161
[*See also Index to Municipal Program pp.* 318–323]

Index

PAGE

American Municipal System
    (see also State Supervision of Cities
        Bad City Government
        Democracy
        Special Interests)
    Summary of 44–49
    No system at all . . . 44 *et seq.*, Chap. X.
    Historical causes of 34–37
    Effect of Spoils System . . . 37–40, 45–6
    Effect of domination of State Legislature, Chap.
        III. (see also State Supervision)
    Compared with foreign . 10–12; Chap. IV., 141–2
    Failure of, not a failure of democracy 10–12, 46–49
    Confusion of policy-determining and administrative functions 45
    Electoral methods must be changed . 181 *et seq.*
        (see Electoral Methods)
    Cities under, in general
        Ill-governed 10–11
        Not self-governing . . . 11, 80
        Foreign experience not applied . 10–12, 65–6
        Problems of, came unawares . . 65–6
        Hopeful signs 77–82
Bad City Government
    (see also Good City Government
        Electoral Methods
        State Supervision)
    Causes of 10
    Not the result of democracy . . 10–11, 200
    In England and Europe 3
    In the United States
        (see American Municipal System)
Ballots
    (see Electoral Methods)
Board of Directors
    (see Texas Plan
        English Municipal Code)
Boss, the

[*See also Index to Municipal Program, pp.* 318–323]

Index

Boss—*Continued*   PAGE
    (see also Special Interests)
    His origin 195
    Inevitable under present system . . . 195–6
Boston Charter
    Outline of proposed new . . . 108–113
    cf. outlines of Municipal Program . . 234–37
"Business Principles"
    In city government, Chap. VIII.

Centralization of Power
    (see Brooklyn Idea
        Texas Idea
        English Municipal Code)
Charters
    (see also Frames of Government
            Home-made Charters)
    Should be mere outlines 188
    Essentials of, Chap. XIV.
Checks and Balances
    (see also English Municipal System)
    Origin of theory 56–7, 71–2
    Wrong in city government . . . 54–6, 83
    Imbedded in constitutions 56
    How avoided by people . . 51–2, 58–60
        (see also Democracy)
Citizen and City, Chap. X.
    (see Self-Government)
City and State
    (see State and City)
"City Government Is Business not Politics"
    (see Chap. VIII.)
City Government *Is* Government
    (see also Political Side
            Self-Government
            English Municipal Code)
    Fundamental . . . Chap. VIII., 9, 153, 155
    Ignored in America
        (see State Supervision)
    Appreciated abroad
    [*See also Index to Municipal Program, pp.* 318–323]

Index

                (see English Municipal Code)
City Legislature
      (see Local Legislation)
City Officials as Agents of State . . .   166, 168–9
      (see also State Supervision
            Self-Government)
Civic Patriotism
      (see Self-Government
           Electoral Methods)
Classification of Cities   143
      (see also State Supervision)
Constitutional Limitations
      (see also Democracy, Advance of)
      Use of . . . . . 71–3, 172, 87 *et seq.*
      How circumvented 144–5
      Significant results of, in Illinois . . . 88–91
Council, City
      (see English Municipal Code
           Self-Government
           cf. Newport Plan)

Debt Limit
      (see Index to Municipal Program)
Democracy
      (see also English Municipal System
           Good City Government)
      Definition of 10–11
      Principles not forms important 10–11, 169–70, 198–9
      More nearly approximated in English cities than
          American 51
      Responsible for good city government abroad . 10–12
      Not responsible for American municipal failure
                            10–12, 46–9
      Does not prevent efficiency, Chap. XVI.
      The real opponents of, Chap. XV.
      The city the battle-ground of, Chap. XV.
      Advance of
           Weapons of 174
           Greatest political force in England and

[*See also Index to Municipal Program, pp.* 318–323]

Democracy—*Continued*
    America for a century . . 50–51
    Effect of written constitutions and statutes upon. . . 50–54, 57–60, 71–4
    Illustrations of . . . 52–3, 174–6
    Effect of certain doctrines on, Chap. V.
    Certain impediments to, Chap. V.

Direct Legislation
  (see Initiative)

Distribution of Powers
  (see Checks and Balances
     Political Side
     Administrative Side)

Efficiency in City Government
  (see also Merit Principle
     Chap. XVI.)

Elective Offices
  (see also Electoral Methods)
  Too numerous 159–60
  Should not include administrative . . . 161
    (cf. Boston Charter, Newport Plan, New York Charter)

Electoral Methods
  (see also Partisanship
     Elective Offices
     Separation of Elections)
  Importance of 149
  Outline of correct 182–3, 185–7
  Present methods
    Mere shams 194–5
    Origin of 54–6
    Especially injurious in city government 68–9
    Promote special interests . 178–9, 186–7
    Voter helpless under 44–6
    Simplification needed . . 57–60, 159–60
     (cf. Boston Charter, Newport Plan)
[*See also Index to Municipal Program, pp.* 318–323]

Index

	PAGE

English Municipal Code
    (see also English Municipal System)
    Fundamentals of 15–25, 39–44
    Operation of 15–25, 39–44
    Council of City under
        Powers of
            Adequate for all local needs . . 15, 16
            Complete over administrative . 16, 18–20
            Coupled with complete responsibility . 19–21
            All powers of city concentrated . 15, 16, 19–21
        Nomination and election of members
            Simple methods 16, 17
            Separated from national . . . 17
        Terms of members 17
    Aldermen
        (see Council)
    Mayor
        (see Council)
    Administrative Service
        Merit principle and efficiency . . . 18
    Concentration of power and responsibility . 19–21
    Democratic results 20, 21
    Compare results in the United States, Chap. IV.; 10–12
    Supervision by Central Government
        Is administrative not legislative . . 21–2
        Efficient, non-political 22–5
        Compare the United States . . . 21–5
    Nominations and Elections
        (see Council)
English Municipal System
    (see also English Municipal Code)
    Successful 3, 6–10, 14–25
    More democratic than American . Chap. IV.; 10–21
    Basic principles of . . . Chaps. II., IV.; 9, 10
    Especially educative for the United States, Chap. IV.
    Before 1835 . . . . 13, 14
        Since 1835 (see English Municipal Code)
    [*See also* Index to Municipal Program, *pp.* 318–323]

Index

PAGE

European Cities
 (see also English Municipal System)
 Basic principles of government in . . . 9, 10
 Well governed 10, 11
 More democratic than American . . 3, 6–10
Executive
 (see also President
   Governor
   Brooklyn Idea)
 Growing trust in 82

Foreign Experience
 (see English Municipal System)
 Not applied 10–12, 65–6
Frame of Government
 (see also Charters)
 Should be made and amended by each city
  for itself 157–8
 Should be simple 159–61
Franchise
 (see Index to Municipal Program
   Electoral Methods
   Public Utilities)

Galveston Plan
 Origin and results of . . . 97–101, 123, 161
Good City Government
 (see also Democracy
   English Municipal System
   Self-Government)
 Basic principles of
   Outlined . Chap. XI.; 4, 5, 7, 9–11, 62–64
   Not impracticable 6, 7
   Successfully applied abroad . 6–8
   Proved by experience at home and
    abroad 10
 Real issue in the fight for 196–7
 In England and Europe 3, 6–10
  (see also English Municipal System)
   Facilitated by general conditions . 61–2
 [See also Index to Municipal Program, pp. 318–323]

Index

Good City Government—*Continued*   PAGE
   In the United States
      Must come through the application of democratic principles . . . 12
      Growing easier of attainment . . 61–2

Good Government
   Fight for, centers in the city, Chap. XV.

"Government by Commission"
   (see also English Municipal Code
      Texas Plan)
   Meaning of . . . . 97 *n*.
   Is democratic . . . . . . 97 *n*.
   Description of 99
   Results of 99–101

Governor
   (see also Democracy)
   Power of, with people 58–60

Growth of Cities
   (see also Self-Government)
   Economic causes of 1–3
   Universality of 2–3
   In the United States . . . 34–37, 65–6
   Vital results of 196–7

Home-Made Charters
   (see also Charters
      Frame of Government)
   Theory of 91–7
   Spread of idea of 93–7

Importance of Good City Government
   (see Chap. XV.)

Independent Voting
   (see also Partisanship)
   In city elections 76–8

Initiative, Referendum, and Recall
   Essence of 105
   Spread of 105–108, 103, 112

[*See also Index to Municipal Program, pp.* 318–323]

Index

PAGE

Judiciary
    (see also Self-Government)
    City should have its own . . . 149–50
Jurisdiction of City
    (see also Self-Government
        State Supervision)
    Need not conflict with State's . 126, 130–31
    Should cover all local matters . . 127–8, 131–2

Legislation for City
    (see Local Legislation
        State Supervision
        Self-Government)
Legislative
    (See also Constitutional Limitations)
    Distrust of 82, 87, 147
Legislative Meddling
    (see State Supervision)
Local Electorate
    (see Self-Government)
Local Legislation
    (see also Self-Government)
    Should be by the city . . . 9, 121, 146–49
    So abroad 9, 10
Local Policy for City
    (see also Self-Government)
    Need of 7, 69
    Subservience to national and state wrong . 69

Machine Government
    (see Special Interests
        State Supervision)
Mayor
    (see also Executive)
    In England
        (see English Municipal Code)
    In the United States
        Concentration of power in . . 82, 84
        "Brooklyn Idea" . . . 84–7, 123

[*See also Index to Municipal Program, pp.* 318–323]

Mayor—*Continued*   PAGE
            (cf. Boston Charter,
                  New York Charter)
Mayor's Veto on State Legislation
      (see also State Supervision)
            In New York 86–7
Merit Principle and System
      (see also Administrative Service)
            Definition of 66
            Growth of, in America 66–8, 110
            Great need of, in cities . . . 68–9, 158–9
            Comment on the proposed new . . . 123–4
Municipal Reform Act of 1835
      (see English Municipal Code)

Newport Charter
Newport Plan
            Outline of 101–105
Nominations
      (see Electoral Methods)

Partisanship, National and State
      (see also Electoral Methods
                  State Supervision)
            Origin of 70–75
            Historical intensity of 70, 75
            Should be excluded from city elections . 158–60
            Effect upon cities 69–70
            Cooling of 75–6
Political or Policy-Determining Side of Government
      (see also Government is Government)
            Necessary to any government . . . 4, 9–10
            Involves divisive partisan issues . 4, 115–16, 121
            Distinction between, and Administrative Side
                        Exists in all government . . . 5, 6
                        Especially important in city government . . Chap. VIII.; 5, 6, 198–200
                        Fundamental 4, 5
                        Growing appreciation of 61, 62, 68–9, 79, 80
      [*See also Index to Municipal Program, pp.* 318–323]

Index

                                                              PAGE

Political Side of Government—*Continued*
    Recognized abroad 63–4
    Illustrated by analogy of private
        business 5, 6

Politicians
  (see Special Interests
      Boss)

Politics
  Definition of 116
  (see also Political Side)

Popular Government
  (see Democracy)

President
  (see also Executive
        Governor)
  Power of, with people 58–60

Privilege
  (see Special Interests)

Public Opinion
  (see also Democracy)
  Need and power of . . Chap. XII.; 172–74

Public Utilities
  (see Franchise)
  City, not special interests, should control . . 193–4

Recall 105–108
  (see Initiative)
  A peculiar form of 112
Referendum 105–108
  (see Initiative)
Responsible Public Officials
  (see Electoral Methods)

Self-Government for Cities
  (see also State Supervision
        English Municipal System)
  Pre-requisites of, Chap. XI.
  Greater degree of, must come, Chap. X.
  Impossible under present electoral methods . 181–4
[*See also Index to Municipal Program, pp.* 318–323]

Index

Self-Government for Cities—*Continued*   PAGE
    City should have a local policy . . 7, 69, 121
    And adequate power to meet all local needs
        125-6, 155-6, 189-90
    Local self-government the corner-stone of our
        institutions 184
Separation of Elections 161-66
    (see also Partisanship
        Electoral Methods)
Special Interests
    (see also Democracy
        Boss)
    Power over city government . . . 192, 194-5
    Favored by charter forms . . . 190-91
    Opposed to all democracy . . . 192
Special Laws
    (see State Supervision)
Spoils System
    (see Partisanship
        State Supervision)
State and City
    (see also State Supervision
        Self-Government)
    Relation a dual one 125
        (*a*) City as local government . . **125**, 132-3
        (*b*) City as agent of State . . 133 *et seq*.
        Compared with Nation and State . 130
State Laws
    (see also State Supervision)
    Proper scope of 156-7
    Enforcement of, by city 133-39
State Supervision of Cities
    (see also Jurisdiction
        State Laws
        Partisanship
        State and City)
    Should be administrative, not legislative
        9, 21-5, Chap. III., 135, 166-8; cf. 112-13

[*See also Index to Municipal Program, pp.* 318-323]

State Supervision of Cities—*Continued*
    Should not extend to details of administration
        135-7, 153-5
    In England
        (see English Municipal Code)
    In the United States
        Wide scope of, Chap. III.
        Compared with English . . 10-12, 31-2
        Amounts to an injurious domination of
            City by State; causes, evils, extent
            of . Chap. III.; 79-81, 125, 135-7, 142-56
Superfluous Legislation 132
    (see also State Supervision)

Texas Plan
    (see Galveston Plan
        Government by Commission)
Town Meeting Plan
    (see Newport Plan)
    [*See also Index to Municipal Program, pp.* 318-323]

INDEX TO MUNICIPAL PROGRAM

	PAGE
Abattoirs, powers of cities as to	264–5
Accounts, Municipal	226–33, 273–4
Uniformity of	249–50
State audit of	228, 273
Actions by citizens	219, 301–2
Administrative Functions	
Separated from Political	209, 216–17
Administrative offices	
Terms not fixed	210–11, 292
Administrative service	
(see also Merit Principle)	
Merit principle in	213, 278 et seq.
Framed by Council	210, 296
Annexation of territory to cities	261–3
Assessment powers of cities	269–70
Ballot	
Form of	217, 243
Secrecy of	243
Bookkeeping, municipal	226–33, 249–50, 273–74
Budget	
Submitted by Mayor	211, 277
Changed by Council	211, 277
Budget of city	277
Charters	
Powers of cities as to	252–5
(see also Home-Made Charters)	
Cities frame their own	234, 252–5

[See also Index, pp. 305–317]

Index to Municipal Program

	PAGE
Cities, powers of	251–2, 263 *et seq.*
City as agent of state	209, 274
City as a local government	207–09
City under municipal program	234–37
Civil service of city	278 *et seq.*
Civil-service commissioners	278–9
Powers of investigation of	285–6
Records of	284–5
Reports of	282
Civil-service regulations	278 *et seq.*
(see also Merit Principle)	
Penalties for violation of	287–91
Illegal payments under	284
Constitutional Amendments	243
Table of contents of	241
Contracts by cities	268–9
Controller	
Elected by Council	210–13, 298–301
Powers of	211–12, 299 *et seq.*
Removed by Council	212, 298
Why not appointed by Mayor?	212
Non-partisan position of	212
Supervises accounts of city	212, 298–301
Supervises accounts of grantees of franchises	221–22, 245, 299
Council	
Composition of	210, 297–8
Elected	209, 293
Elects its own officers	294
Elects controller,	298
Establishes municipal offices	296
Fixes its own rules	294
Judge of election of its members subject to review by the courts	293
Meetings of	294–5
Powers of	210
Powers of appropriation	296–7
Powers of investigation	210–11, 296
Powers of taxation	296–7

[*See also Index, pp.* 305–317]

Council—*Continued* PAGE
    Quorum 294
    Removes controller 298
Councillors
    Election and terms of . . . 210, 292–93
Courts, city
    Created by city 206, 250, 266
    Jurisdiction of 206–07, 250, 266

Debts
    What included in debt limit . 222–25, 245–48
Direct legislation . . . 218–19, 248–49, 297–98
Dock powers 264

Elections
    Simplicity of 216–18, 296
    Separation from state and national . 216–18, 302
Elective officers
    Councillors and Mayor only . . . 209, 251
English Cities
    Government of, outlined 213–14
    Municipal Program in part modelled upon 214–17

Ferries, wharves, docks, streets, etc. 220–22, 244–45, 267–68
    Inalienability of . . 220–22, 244–45, 267–68
Ferry powers 264
Financial reports
    By cities to state 227, 249
    What they should contain . . 227–32, 249–50
Franchises
    (see also Public Utilities)
    Grants of 220–21, 244–45
    Powers of city as to 220, 267–68
    Inalienability of 220, 244–45
    Accounts of grantees of . . . 221–22, 245
    Reports by grantees of 221–22

General laws
    Defined 208
    Affecting city, unrestricted . . . 205, 208
General ticket, election of Council by . . . 293
    [*See also Index, pp.* 305–317]

Index to Municipal Program

	PAGE
Good city government	
Outline of	234–37
Harbor powers	264
Heads of departments	
Appointed by Mayor	210, 278
At Council meetings.	276
Home-made charters	233–34, 252–55
Incorporation of cities	208, 252, 260–61
Indebtedness	
Power of city to incur .	222–25, 245–48, 270–72
Initiative	218–19
Investigations	210–11, 292, 296
Judicial officers of city	206–07, 250, 266
Market powers	264
Mayor	
Attendance at Council meetings . . .	276
Budget prepared by	211, 277
Compensation fixed by Council . . .	278
Elected	209, 251
Messages to Council	211, 277
Powers of	210–11, 214
Power of appointment	251, 278
Power of investigation	292
Power of removal . . .	210, 251, 291–92
Removal of, by governor . . .	211, 276
Suspension of, by governor	211
Term of	211, 275
Vacancy in office how filled . . .	275
Veto power of	276–7
Merit system	213, 251, 278–92
Minority representation . . .	248–49, 297–98
Municipal Corporations Act	260
Table of contents of	256
Municipal organization	250–51

[*See also Index, pp.* 305–317]

322   Index to Municipal Program

Municipal organization—*Continued* PAGE
    Determined by Council 296
Municipal Program
    Origin of 203–04
    General divisions of 204–05
    City under 234–37
    Summary of 234–37

National Municipal League
    Origin of 203
Nomination of city officers
    In general 217–18, 243–44
    By petition 243–44, 303–04

Officers, terms of, not fixed 210–11, 292
Ordinance, powers of 264

Penal powers 265
Petitions 255, 303–04
Petition, nomination by . . 217–18, 243–44, 303–04
Powers of the city . . . . . 205 *et seq.*
    Sufficient for all local functions . . 207–08
    Limitations upon 205–06
    (see Cities; special Legislation)
Private bills 244
Proportional representation . . . 248–49, 297–98
Public utilities 205
    Control of . 219–22, 244–45, 251–52, 263, 267–68
    (see Franchises)

Recall 218–19
Referendum 218–19
Registration of voters 217–18, 243

Schools, power of cities over 265
Secrecy in voting 217, 243
Self-supporting enterprises
    Bonds for, not included in debt limit . 222–25, 246–47
Sewer powers 264
Sinking funds 225–26, 247
Special legislation
    Defined 205–06

[*See also Index, pp.* 305–317]

Index to Municipal Program

Special legislation—*Continued*	PAGE
How enacted	205–06, 251–52
City's veto power upon	205–06, 252
State and city	
Relation of	208–09
State interference	
With cities, restricted	207–08, 274
Structural plan of city government outlined	214–16
Taxation	
Powers of cities over	205, 269
Tax rate	270–72
Territory, annexation of	261–63
Trusts	232–33
Uniform accounting	249–50
(see Accounts)	
Veto power	
Of Mayor	276–77
Of city	
(see Special Legislation)	
Water-works	264
Wharf powers	264

[*See also Index, pp.* 305–317]

Fe 4 '16

OCT 14

OCT 10

MAY 1

MAY 15